OTHER BOOKS
BY RAMONA RICHARDS

Fiction

Burying Daisy Doe (coming 2020)
Murder in the Family
Memory of Murder
House of Secrets
Field of Danger
The Taking of Carly Bradford
The Face of Deceit
A Murder Among Friends

Devotionals

My Mother's Quilts
Secrets of Confidence
A Moment with God for Single Parents

Contributor

Let the Earth Rejoice
So God Made a Dog
Just Breathe
Trusting Jesus Every Day
God's Provision in Tough Times
Fulfilled: The NIV Devotional Bible for Single Women
Wonderfully Made
Heavenly Humor for the Dieter's Soul

TRACKING CHANGES

One Editor's Advice to
Inspirational Fiction Authors

RAMONA RICHARDS

NEW HOPE™
PUBLISHERS
Imprint of Iron Stream Media
Birmingham, Alabama

New Hope® Publishers
100 Missionary Ridge
Birmingham, AL 35242
An imprint of Iron Stream Media
IronStreamMedia.com
NewHopePublishers.com

Iron Stream Media serves its authors as they express their views, which may not express the views of the publisher.

Library of Congress Cataloging-in-Publication Data

Names: Richards, Ramona, 1957- author.
Title: Tracking changes : one editor's advice to inspirational fiction authors / Ramona Richards.
Description: Birmingham, Alabama : New Hope Publishers, 2020.
Identifiers: LCCN 2020006166 (print) | LCCN 2020006167 (ebook) | ISBN 9781563094163 (trade paperback) | ISBN 9781563094170 (epub)
Subjects: LCSH: Christian fiction—Authorship.
Classification: LCC PN3377.5.C47 R53 2020 (print) | LCC PN3377.5.C47 (ebook) | DDC 808.06/623—dc23
LC record available at https://lccn.loc.gov/2020006166
LC ebook record available at https://lccn.loc.gov/2020006167

ISBN-13: 978-1-56309-416-3
Ebook ISBN: 978-1-56309-417-0

1 2 3 4 5—24 23 22 21 20

This one is for
Bonnie S. Calhoun
Because you said, "Yes, you can."

CONTENTS

Contents

Just One Editor's Opinion

I honestly don't know how it happened. I'd been working with author and editor Bonnie Calhoun on a book for Abingdon Press during the time I was the acquisitions editor there. We frequently had these interminable conversations that sometimes happen between editor and author, and in the midst of one of them, we talked about the columns she featured in *Christian Fiction Online Magazine*. I don't remember if she offered or I asked. Maybe both. But the next thing I know, we're discussing the parameters of a column called Track Changes, after that nefarious Microsoft Word feature that authors and editors use to communicate with each other.

For the next four years, I wrote a monthly column for Bonnie, exploring the world of publishing from an acquisition editor's side of the desk. After the column—and, unfortunately, her online magazine—ended, I continued to post about writing on a variety of blogs, including my own. Finally, I began thinking about gathering the articles into a book. Since the archived columns aren't available to the general public, I thought it might be nice to have the most popular ones in one place. I've expanded

some of the entries, and I've written several new essays to round out the areas I get asked about at conferences. A number of writers have mentioned that my advice helped them. I hope it continues to help others as well. So...who am I to be blithely handing out advice to authors?

Well, I'm an author myself. And an editor. I've been doing both a long time.

As a writer of nonfiction, I placed my first article (a biographical sketch of a small-town historical figure) when I was a junior in high school. I went on to write and sell everything from sales training videos to book reviews and short stories. I've written articles for major magazines, and I've ghostwritten business fables. My first book, a collection of devotions, led me to write devotions for numerous publication, and in 2016, Worthy Publishing released *My Mother's Quilts*, a collection of devotions about the thirty quilts I inherited from my mother. I've contributed other devotions to several collections...and one Bible.

As a writer of fiction, I sold my first short story in 1986, and as of 2020, I've sold eight novels, with more in the works.

As an editor, my first position was with the children's book division of Abingdon Press, and I went on to be an in-house editor for *Ideals* magazine and several Christian trade book lines. I've edited Bibles and curriculum for Thomas Nelson, and in 2010, I returned to Abingdon to edit their fiction line. Once, when I was freelancing, I even edited a series of air conditioning repair manuals.

Oh, and I've taught English at the college level. English is my first love and my ongoing profession, in whatever form that takes.

Yet I am still just one editor with one point of view. Other editors will have different opinions. House styles differ, and some rely on the *Chicago Manual of Style* or *The Christian Writer's Manual of Style*, while others use the AP stylebook or an academic or profession-specific style book. English is a wonderful, ever-evolving language. That it can be used in so many diverse ways is one of its beauties.

Publishing also changes rapidly, especially now. I've updated sections wherever possible, but this remains a book focused on traditional publishing paths and the relationships between authors and editors. I touch on self-publishing occasionally, but resources in that area are plentiful in other arenas. I've made suggestions and lists of references in the back of the book.

As I used to tell my English students, "I'm old. I've done a lot of stuff." And I've learned a little along the way from a lot of wise people. Time to share some of that.

I've divided the book into two parts. The first one focuses on the art and craft of writing and editing as well as the relationships of writers to editors. The second part is on what happens *after* the manuscript is complete and after you place it with a publisher.

I hope you can take away something from these pages that will help you in your writing and your career.

Ramona
January 2020

Part One

The Writing Life: Art, Craft, Frustration, and Perseverance

WHATEVER IS GOOD

*Employ whatever God has entrusted you with, in doing good,
all possible good, in every possible kind and degree.*

John Wesley

This quotation from John Wesley may have been inspired by 1 Peter 4:10, which instructs us in a similar fashion: "God has given each of you a gift from his great variety of spiritual gifts. Use them well to serve one another."

Most of us recognize that our ability to string words together in a skilled way is a gift from God, one that we should use to the best of our ability to honor Him and be a good manager of that gift. But therein lies the rub...that most indeterminate and relative of words: "good."

What does that mean in terms of our writing? What did Peter mean, what did Wesley mean, by "doing good," being a "good manager"? Not in any deep theological sense but in a practical, everyday, "how do I make the best choices" sense.

- **Never take your gift for granted.** Writers often hang out with a lot of other writers. Our friends tend to be smart as well, and occasionally we drift into this place where we believe anyone could do what we do with a little training. Especially after so many rejections, we begin to doubt our gift. This is *so not* the truth. You have a *gift* unique to you. Only you can nourish it, strengthen it, and tell the stories you are meant to tell.

- **You do need to nourish your gift**, strengthen it, by writing and learning continually. Your gift came from God with raw potential, like an athlete's gift for running or throwing a ball. *Receiving the gift is just the beginning.* Take courses, listen to other authors, read as much as you can in your genre or chosen field. Your gift is like possessing a foreign language: if you don't use it, it will grow weak and stale.

- **Make choices that honor the Gift Giver.** You may be a whiz at dialogue and human psychology. This doesn't mean you should write the next *Fifty Shades of Grey*. And I don't mean to just avoid pornography—there are many ways to write, and you have claimed the label of Christian. You may be the only reflection of Christ some people will see. Keep that in mind when stringing your words together.

- **Be flexible and listen to the Lord.** Since He gave you the gift, He has a plan for you and a path for you to walk with it. You may crave writing romance novels, but He may lead you to writing suspense or devotionals, which require as much a gift for storytelling as a novel.

In fact, repeat that to yourself: ***Since He gave you the gift, He has a plan for you to use it.*** And the best way to know that plan is to listen

and to watch for the doors He opens. Don't ignore them; they're there for a reason. A "good" reason.

When you keep your writing eyes on **Him**, "good" becomes clear.

ARE YOU A
CYFARWYDDION?

Whoever tells the story, shapes the culture.

Plato

Don't worry about looking up that word. I'll get to it in a minute.

A few years ago, one of the Abingdon Press authors I worked with, Krista Phillips, posted a blog about marketing and the inner conflicts we sometimes have about selling our own work. As Christians, we are taught to embrace humility and to reject bragging, especially about ourselves.

Yet, as writers, we also believe that God has gifted us with a unique voice and a heart for telling great stories, ones that embrace His Word. We feel called to share His message with others, just as He directed us to do. We remember that He shared His lessons in the form of parables, and that storytelling is something that resonates in all our hearts.

More than some folks might want to believe. I sometimes hear from people who "never read fiction—those stories are just made up." Oh, what they're missing! Because centuries before nonfiction books clustered on library shelves, back when the world was lit only by fire, our history, our heroes, our faith, and our traditions were passed on, generation to generation, by storytellers.

You, each and every one of you, are one of their heirs.

In almost every language, there's a special word (often more than one) for the guest who was revered, welcomed, and embraced around every hearth. The guest who passed on the news from the next town, shared ancient legends, and taught lessons through the stories of adventures and great quests.

Skald

Rhapsode

Minstrel

Scop

Seanachie

Cyfarwyddion

And that's just a few. The word most of us know—bard—was a particular class of poet storyteller, usually connected with one household, supported by the lord of the land. The bard committed to composing verses that passed on history, tales, and legends of the household. Other, less lofty (and less compensated) storytellers committed to memory prodigious numbers of tales. In one Celtic tradition, a potential storyteller spent at least twelve to fifteen years learning and reciting, putting more than 250

primary stories and 100 secondary stories to memory, ready to share at anytime.

That's a lot to keep in mind. In the case of the Welsh *cyfarwyddion*, this contributed to the creation of the Triads, which made easy memory cues. Storytellers used them to remember kings, battles, heroic tales ("The Three Chieftains of Arthur's Court" or "The Three Battle-Leaders"), but they would also have Triads that passed on common wisdom. One of my favorites: "Three things to be controlled above all others: The hand, the tongue, desire." Words that will sound familiar if you've ever read James 3.

Storytelling is, if you will, a part of our cultural DNA.

Like many writers, I come from a long line of storytellers. As a kid, I perched on my grandfather's knee and listened to a bunch of folks who'd just spent their days in the fields tell one story after another, most of them full of fun and pranks, with lessons hanging barely beneath the surface. When I grew up, I turned all intellectual and pretentious, and wrote such pieces as *In the Image of Our Fathers: Formulaic Heroes as Classic Myths*—a grand title for a master's thesis that compared modern genre heroes to the classic quest myth.

In other words, Louis L'Amour's tales of the Sacketts bear a great resemblance to Beowulf—and the travels and travails of the Bible heroes. Are there any greater adventures than that of Paul's shipwreck or David's battles? (I've always said that if you really want to bring children to Scripture, wait about teaching them John and start with 1 and 2 Samuel.)

So what does all this rambling about storytelling have to do with marketing a book?

You have two gifts from two traditions. One of words. One of faith. You also have the directive to share your faith with as many people as possible. Your gift and your biggest opportunity to do that is with your words.

Fiction may be entertaining, just as the stories of the *cyfarwyddion* were. But the lessons are always, always "hanging barely beneath the surface." So whether you're gathered around a fire or curled up in a recliner, if you're reading or writing, you're in the process of sharing our traditions, our history, and our faith.

So marketing a book is not bragging. It's taking your light out from under a bushel.

WHAT KIND OF WRITER ARE YOU? I'M A WRITER.

There is no greater agony than bearing an untold story inside you.

Maya Angelou

I 'm about to write something that may be a bit controversial, and you are free to disagree with me. But if I hear the question that every writer gets, usually from other writers, again, I may become violent.

"You write? Are you a plotter or a pantser?"

My answer: "Neither. I'm a writer."

I would like to posit for you to consider that there is no "plotter vs. pantser" process of working. Those are arbitrary labels for the way we construct our stories, and they are detrimental to your identification as a writer. They attempt to *prescribe* what you do, and if you adopt one, you can find that it limits your freedom to work.

Here's why.

We are storytellers. First and foremost. Nonfiction or fiction, doesn't matter. If you have a drive to write, if you *crave* getting words on paper, then you are a storyteller. And stories come to us in a million ways. We find them in dreams, in abandoned cars, in garbage bins, family conflicts, news reports, science projects. Sometimes they appear in our heads fully formed, other times piecemeal, with one incident at a time coming to us in the shower or at a red light.

And they all start with the big question: **What if?**...

What if...you found a body in your backseat when you came out to go to work? **What if**...your sister's illness had taken a different direction? **What if**...

A story that comes to you in its entirety might be better scribbled down as fast as possible, writing organically (a word I prefer to "pantser" anyway), the events tumbling out of your head as fast as you can type. One that is centered on a larger "what if?" might be better outlined with index cards, Post-it Notes, or an Excel spreadsheet (plotted), mostly because all the "connective tissue" of the story isn't in place in your head yet.

In other words, **your method should match the story**, not the person.

I have talked to far too many "organic" writers who have stalled out in a story because they never learned to or grew comfortable with plotting. I've known "plotters" who get all their big scenes worked out, then they lose the drive for the tale because...well... the story's now been told. They don't have a sense of the organic

to go back and let the connective tissue grow and flow around the scenes.

And I've experienced both.

For many years, I claimed the "pantser" label, and I stalled out in many a tale, especially before I learned how to edit fiction. I tried detailed plotting but found I had no impetus *at all* to continue writing once the story was told. Because one of the publishers I write for demands a lengthy, detailed synopsis, I found myself working with a combination of the two "labels." Now I start with a type of annotated outline (also known as a synopsis), but not so detailed that I lose the story craving. I don't "plot," per se, but I know a great more about where I'm going with the tale...enough that I catch those painted corners before they come around.

Which has led me to having some intimate, whispered conversations with authors unwilling to claim one of those prescribed labels. Which is why I'm now in the mood to start a revolution.

You are not a plotter. You do not write organically.

You're a writer. Period. You have spent years studying your craft. You understand goal, motivation, conflict; plot points; denouement. You read extensively in every genre. You know the expectations and basic elements of your own genre. You have developed an almost intuitive feel for the language. You are disciplined and determined to succeed. You claim that inner beast that pushes you to put words into sentences, nurturing and embracing it. You are flexible enough to let the process fit the story that is tumbling out of your heart.

You cannot...can NOT...summarize that with a single label about the process of creating a book.

You are a storyteller. You are a writer. Embrace and acknowledge all that entails.

A WRITER?
WHY ME, LORD?

High mastery is expected of symphony musicians, ballerinas, Olympic athletes, brain surgeons and more. Why not novelists too?

Donald Maass

Why do you write? Think about that for a few moments.

I lead a split life. On one hand, I'm an editor, and I've worked at this profession since 1981. Before that, I corrected friends' term papers in college, and everyone thought I would be a teacher or professor.

I'm also a writer. I've been doing that since I was a kid, and I first published at seventeen. It's as much a part of me as my eye color. I have to write just as I have to breathe. If I stop, my whole world goes wacky, and friends start asking odd questions like, "Have you written anything lately?" There are some days it feels more like a curse than a blessing.

Most of all, I'm a reader. That obviously predates the writing, but not by as much as you might think. I started reading at five, and the drive to write was so strong that my brother had to explain to me the meaning of the word "plagiarism" when I was seven and he found me hand-copying a biography of Daniel Boone. "You have to make up your own," he said. So I did.

As a reader, I cut my literary teeth on YA mysteries and science fiction, which held sway until I was twelve. That's when I read my first adult book, Catherine Marshall's *Christy*. Biographies and real-life adventure stories lined my shelves. My best friend in high school was also a reader, and together we sought out the best we could find: Mary Stewart, Victoria Holt, Robert Heinlein, Harlan Ellison. We wanted to be challenged, fascinated, enthralled. We often asked the librarian, "Who should we read next?" We wanted the best.

I wanted to write like them, and I struggled for years to find my own voice. I didn't want to be *them*; my goal was to be *the best*.

So to this day, I'm startled when I hear writers whose goals sound like: "I want to do three books a year. I don't have time for quality" or "I think my writing is good enough for such-and-such a publisher." Even worse? "My readers don't have high expectations. What I do is good enough."

Wow. You have no idea how sad these concepts make me. On so many levels. And I have heard them more times than I care to count.

Don't get me wrong. I know all too well what it is to be a "working writer," one who has to make a living with words. When your

words pay the bills, you'll take just about any job that pays. And a working writer has to treat art like a business with defined productivity goals. Not only is there nothing wrong with that, I'd encourage it.

But quantity is not a substitute for quality. Shouldn't be. *Ever.*

What would you think if you heard the electrician working on your house say, "Oh, that's good enough. They'll never notice the difference"?

I don't know about you, but I'd be hiring another electrician. Preferably the best I could find.

If you write Christian fiction, then you probably already know you write in a literary ghetto. Folks outside our slice of the publishing industry view us askance, since their ideas of Christian fiction still languishes under the impressions created by scores of horribly written novels in the '70s and '80s. They believe we care more about the message than the medium.

In response to that, some writers have toned back on their message, seeking to become "less preachy." Some hope to write works that cross over to the mainstream market. They want to do more than "preach to the choir."

I believe this is a seriously misguided notion.

The books that *have* crossed over to the mainstream have done so not because of their lack of "preachiness." They've done so because **they are the best of their kind.**

Some market decisions a writer *must* make. You need to decide on your genre, for instance, and your voice. But if you try to be a

mugwump—a fence-sitter with your mug on one side and your wump on the other—then you're most likely going to miss out on reaching the very readers you hope to.

As an editor, I'm not just looking for a great historical romance. I'm looking for the best one out of all the submissions that cross my desk. The one that catches my attention and proves to me that not only does this author know what she's doing with this genre, but she's determined to write the best book she possibly can.

Focus on becoming the best writer you can be. Study your chosen genre carefully. Focus on the details, the expectations of that genre, the audience. Read the best writers in it, both Christian fiction and mainstream.

Then fight. Work and fight to be the best mystery writer. The finest women's fiction author. The leading suspense novelist. The greatest romance author.

Stop second-guessing the market, and don't settle for a lower quality just because you think it's "good enough." Write the books you want to write with the greatest quality you can produce. Success will follow.

Don't just be your best. Be *the* best.

WRITE WHAT YOU... *WHAT?*

Write what you know. That should leave you with a lot of free time.

Howard Nemerov

We've all heard it. I've heard it attributed to Mark Twain, which makes me raise an eyebrow. After all, about half his well-known quotations were said with a certain sardonic nature. (The other half aren't actually his, but that's another story. Mr. Sam gets mistaken for Will Rogers a lot, and vice versa. Quotation sites can be some of the worst sources of misinformation.)

Write what you know.

Meh. This is, without a doubt, the worst possible advice to give to a writer.

First of all, it puts a limit on your imagination. If you're a science fiction writer, for example, you may want to develop an innovative irrigation system for the underground gardens of Titan. I would be surprised if you are a great SF author *and* a hydroponics

expert on underground gardens *and* a qualified astrogeologist with knowledge of the geologic structure of Saturn's moons. Somewhere along the line, you'll need to do some research, then extrapolate from what is known here on earth.

Second, it puts a limit on your love of words. Writers love words. They love the sound of them as they read aloud from their own works. They love the way words ebb and flow through *showing* (not *telling*), revealing Chekhov's famous "glint on glass" instead of "the moon is shining." To limit your writing to things you know puts your vocabulary in a rut of recycled rambling.

Third, it puts a limit on your passion, that uncontrollable urge to scribble, to type madly, to empty your head of the stories that build up in there, each of them fighting for attention like a steam-driven squabble of ADD third graders. As George Orwell said in his well-known essay, "Why I Write":

> *Writing a book is a horrible, exhausting struggle, like a long bout of some painful illness. One would never undertake such a thing if one were not driven on by some demon whom one can neither resist nor understand.*

Here's my interpretation of all this: Don't write what you know. **Write what you love.** If you love love, write romance. If you love unexpectedly finding dead bodies, write mysteries. If you love nonstop action, write thrillers. If you love diving into the unending wormhole of historical research, write about it!

And lest you think I don't take my own advice...I love scuba diving. In 1992, I pursued a long-denied craving and completed several courses, including the one for rescue diver, and to this day I

carry my certification card everywhere I go. I'm proud of it, even if the picture leaves a lot to be desired. (I've had better driver's license photos.) Just as I'd imagined for years, I fell totally in love with being underwater, to the point that I once walked into a glass wall at a major city aquarium, so lost was I in the idea of getting closer to the fish. I just forgot I was on dry land.

What I have *not* done, however, is wreck diving and underwater salvage. And I plan to write about that. I am fascinated by what happens to bodies, cars, buildings, and ships when submerged—especially what happens forensically when one of those items is a part of a crime. I'm not a forensics expert, but that's when *love* becomes *research*.

So my advice is go write your passion, and just let "what you know" be the launch pad for more engaging worlds.

Yes, You Will Be Edited

No passion in the world, no love or hate, is equal to the passion to alter someone else's draft.

H. G. Wells[*]

In 1981, when I'd only been on my first editorial job for a few weeks, I received a letter from a reader that noted a mistake in one of our books. I was horrified. The book had been out for several years, but no one had noticed the text under one of the pictures read: "Joseph had *lead* the donkey to the stable."

I took the letter to my boss, expecting the same shock. After all, this was a children's book. Maybe 1,000 words long. It had been through two edits, a copyedit, and two proofings. Five reprintings, each of which had been proofread. Had been on library shelves for years uncorrected. This should not happen! I expected outrage.

---

[*] This attribution remains unverified but has been commonly accepted as being from Wells. For more information, see https://quoteinvestigator.com/2016/01/04/editing/

Instead, she told me who to send the correction to and went back to work, calm as could be. "But, but, but—" I sputtered.

She smiled. Gently. Understanding. "Lesson number one in this business, Ramona, is that there's no such thing as a perfect book. Once you accept that, your life will be much less stressful."

I often hear from writers who have studied the masters and read Deb Dixon's books until the pages were dog-eared. They've paid for an edit on their baby, or they had their former English teacher correct the grammar. They've worked for years on making their book as perfect as possible. *Obviously* it's perfect; after all, an editor bought it!

Needless to say, they're a little stunned when they get the first edit.

The surprise comes from two assumptions about how editors work:

- how we choose what we buy, and
- how we edit a purchased manuscript.

Assumption One
Editors only buy manuscripts ready to publish.

No matter how often they hear otherwise, writers often cling to the idea that an editor buys a book because it is *perfect*. Perfect story, perfect writing, perfect for the line, perfect for selling. Therefore, it shouldn't need much editing. After all, it's *perfect*.

Uh...no.

We're not looking for "perfect." Editors know that doesn't exist. Humans are flawed, and even great authors get edited, as we

found out a few years ago with Jane Austen. Not even *Bibles* come out perfect, because while the Word was breathed by God, mere humans wrote the notes and did the typesetting and proofreading.

What editors want most is a great story in a unique voice.

Memorize that. Print it out and put it on your fridge. Editors want to be wooed by your story, not the perfection of your grammar or plot structure. Enchant us on the first page with your storytelling capabilities. Only then do we ask the next level of questions:

- Does it fit our program? Do I have a slot for this genre?
- Can I sell it to the acquisitions and marketing team?
- Will it succeed in the marketplace? Can I make the profit and loss statement on it work?
- Is the author interested in a one-shot deal or a career?
- How deep will the edit have to be? (This is where we take note of your ability to use a comma in the right place.)

"Is it perfect?" doesn't even make the list.

Remember: I'm not saying grammar doesn't matter; it does. In fact, it would be hard to enchant an editor completely with that first page if your grammar is truly lousy. And even an enchanted editor will reject a manuscript if she gets to the "deep edit" question and realizes it'll be too hard or take too long to fix the issues. Excellent grammar and structure will *help* you sell. But it's only part of the picture.

You don't sell because your manuscript is perfect and your work is finished. Selling just means you've hit that storytelling sweet spot that every editor longs to discover.

In fact, selling means the hardest part of your work has only just begun.

Assumption Two

A publication edit is identical to a content or grammar edit.

You've sold! Congratulations! Ready for hard part?

Uh...no. You're *not* finished just because you sold. Now comes the first of many rounds of editing. Just remember that writing is solitary. Editing is solitary. But *publishing*—the blending of the two—is a partnership.

But, first, a pause for a few definitions.

Over the past thirty years, I've worked on staff or as a freelancer for about two dozen publishers. All take a fiction manuscript through similar stages, although the stages may have different names and those names may overlap. But they usually flow like this:

1. **The "big picture" edit (also called the macro, content, substantive, or structure edit).** At this stage the editor takes a look at character arcs, plot structure (and the resulting holes), house, line, or genre conventions [such as Happily Ever After endings (HEAs), conversions, timelines, faith elements, or endgame weddings]. This is when such comments arise as:

   - Is the dark moment a true abyss or just a wrong turn?
   - Why didn't you finish subplot A?
   - Too much backstory in chapter one, and your first plot point arrives way too soon.
   - Why did Sally disappear after page 240?

- There's too much sexual chemistry between your heroine and the hero's sidekick.
- Why is your heroine's sister pregnant for 18 months? (yes, it happens)

2. **The "detail" edit (also called the line, content, substantive, or copyedit).** This is when the manuscript is read for details such as changing eye color, fact vs. fiction details, corrections made after the "big picture," etc. This is when you'll get such comments as:

- Chevrolet didn't make a Corvette that year, and never with a 2-cylinder engine.
- Unless he's Superman, Jeff won't really be able to pick up a piece of granite the size of a car engine without a little help.
- I'm not sure any coastal area of Louisiana could be considered "arid."
- The "west coast" of Florida is a local description that doesn't include the panhandle. It's different from "the Gulf coast," and they aren't interchangeable.
- Why is your heroine's sister still pregnant for 18 months?

3. **The "picky" edit (also called the line, copy, or content edit).** This is when such things as pacing, grammar, passive voice, etc., are addressed. This is when the manuscript may look like a truck ran over it, and you'll wonder if you forgot how to write or why they bought the nasty thing in the first place.

Once these editorial steps are complete, your manuscript will be sent to typesetting, and the proofreading stages begin. Some publishers combine stages 1 and 2; some combine 2 and 3. Some

add a fourth, just to be sure, especially if your heroine's sister hasn't had that baby yet.

Take a breath. Maybe a cold drink. And don't give up.

A good fiction editor will be your friend and ally. Her job is to work with you to make your book the best it can be. To make *your* book in *your* voice soar higher and further for the readers than you had ever hoped. She's trained to see the "big picture" that you, as the author, may not be able to because of either lack of experience or unfamiliarity with a publisher's line and house style. (And, no, the Oxford comma is not universal.)

Try to remember that the number of good fiction editors in the US is very small. In terms of other professions, even editorial professions, it's extremely small. There might be around 500 of us. Maybe. Especially those who can handle a "big picture" edit. And I can count the number of "picky" editors I trust with a novel on one hand.

We do this not just because we love books and words but because we love *fiction*. And want yours to fly.

Unless they're trained in the field or are published novelists, English teachers don't usually make good fiction editors. The same with nonfiction editors or proofreaders who work for the local paper. They cannot make your book "perfect." In fact, I had to learn the hard way that excellent nonfiction editors can, in fact, be detrimental to a novel—I've been known to strip a manuscript of all edits after such an event and start from scratch.

So...yes, you will be edited, probably more than you expected. But also don't be afraid to question changes that you feel go too

far. The key is to remember who your readers are. Will the edit help you reach them and keep you from tripping them out of the story? Does it make your book better or just different?

It's a give and take. Partner with your editor. Then go on to write the next book. After all, she's waiting for it.

HOW AN EDITOR (NOT A GRAMMAR NAZI) IS BORN

If when we are taught English we are just taught the rules of grammar, it would take all our love of our language away from us. What makes us love a subject like English is when we learn all these fantastic stories. Feeding the imagination is what makes a subject come alive.

Daniel Tammet

Confession time: Hi, I'm Ramona. I used to be a Grammar Nazi.

Chorus: *Hi, Ramona.*

Confession time: Then I became an editor.

Chorus: *Say what?*

In a fair land far away (Tennessee in the '70s), I majored in English. Twice. The first time I had a minor in Modern European Studies (multiple classes in history, politics, and foreign languages) and an emphasis in grammar and composition. I took

advanced classes in both. I can diagram sentences from James Joyce (yes, that was one of the exercises). I loved it.

Repeat that. *Loved it.* Correct grammar became a passion. People were afraid to write me letters. I was a grammar dictator. The only literature classes I took were medieval and modern. I preferred studying the history of the English language to historical classics.

In fact, my advisor finally took me aside and told me that if I didn't take a class in eighteenth-century literature, he wouldn't let me graduate. I did, but oh-my-word-*boring*. I couldn't wait to get out of it and back to my jots and tittles. (To this day I have little use for any author who wrote between 1700 and 1920, except for Twain and Dumas.)

The second time, for my masters degree, I had to take a foreign language. German. Which taught me even *more* about grammar (German and English have similar Indo-European roots). By the time those degrees were in hand, I had Harbrace, and Turabian, and the *Chicago Manual of Style*, and Strunk & White *memorized*. I had a red pen grafted to my left hand. I was *ready for publishing*.

Then...I actually got a job in publishing. Working with children's books. And here are the first two lessons I learned in publishing:

1. What makes a good children's book is the same thing that make a good adult book: story. (J. K. Rowling, anyone?) Story is king.
2. There's no such thing as a perfect book.

These two have served me well. Thirty-plus years down the pike, I still remember that first letter of correction from a reader. I was devastated, even though I'd had nothing to do with the book. It had been published long before I'd even graduated from college.

My boss, however, was quite nonchalant, with her "no such thing as a perfect book" lesson. "Ramona, if you get upset over every mistake in a printed book, you're going to spend your life in a tizzy," she said gently. "Humans make mistakes. And grammar changes."

Wait. What? Grammar *changes*?

Definitely not something I heard back in that fair land far away. I was just beginning to learn how far away it was. I soon began to read publications like *The Editorial Eye*, which covered the ongoing changes in grammar. Now I read grammar blogs. CMOS Q&A pages. I went from being a *pre*scriptivist (one who dictates how grammar *should be* used correctly) to a *de*scriptivist (one who describes how current grammar *is* used correctly). And I discovered that editing content, editing *story*, is far more satisfying to me.

Above all, I began to truly appreciate the overwhelming beauty of this whackadoodle language we call English. It's fluid and flexible with rules that guide yet shift. It allows for different stylebooks to flourish (Associated Press is not CMOS is not APA style, and serial commas are not universal). It allows new words to be added and old words to change or vanish. Words are allowed to *evolve*. Nouns become verbs, and vice versa. *Googol*, a noun, inspired *Google*, a proper noun, which became a verb.

In fiction as well as nonfiction, English allows for the development of an author's voice through selective syntax, dialogue, and dialectal phrasings. And I'm always amused at people who

desperately fight some usages until they're added to the Oxford English Dictionary. Then they're OK, accepted by the "authority" of the OED, which has always been a *descriptivist* publication.

So what's my point?

My point is that every book has mistakes (even if *you* don't catch them), and some grammatical "mistakes" aren't actually mistakes. When reading a book, try focusing on content, on story, not on the occasional trip-up by a copyeditor. **Because if you let a few grammatical mistakes or typos upset your reading of a book, then you are going to overlook some of the most beautiful and well-written (if not well-proofed) books in our language.**

Don't get me wrong; in some ways this attitude (books must be perfect) is helpful to authors and publishers. We do take emails about mistakes seriously, and often readers find things that *should* be corrected. And, once upon a time, complaints about things that are *not*, in fact, wrong used to have little impact. (I once had a woman complain to me about the use of parentheses in the King James Version of the Bible, since nothing in God's word is parenthetical. I had to explain to her the evolution of parentheses as punctuation and that in older versions of the KJV, they were perfectly acceptable.)

But now we have the internet, where a campaign against a mistake can cost an author a career.

Think I'm exaggerating?

A publisher I worked for was startled when they were notified that Amazon had pulled the "Buy" button from one of our books because of *one* reader's complaints about the "mistakes" in the book. They sent us the list. Of all the "mistakes" on this reader's list, one was

a typo. One was a continuity error. The rest weren't mistakes at all but rather out-of-date grammar or the author's voice in dialogue. So, no, these weren't going to be changed, no matter how much one reader protested. They weren't wrong; she was.

But even though this reader was incorrect on most of her complaints, she cost the author sales. And she has a platform to continue to complain. This wasn't justified nitpicking; this was just mean.

So, I beg of you, when you see mistakes in a published book, don't grab a red pen and a platform. Don't wail and jive in Amazon reviews about the lousy copyediting. Be biblical—go straight to the source first. Contact the author or publisher (we're online everywhere these days), and alert them to the problem. Give them a chance to respond.

And if your grammatical knowledge is based on what you learned before 2001, please do not mention split infinitives. They've been acceptable since at least 1983, if not before.

Or to quote a CMOS Q&A column: "In this day and age, it seems, an injunction against splitting infinitives is one of those shibboleths whose only reason for survival is to give increased meaning to the lives of those who can both identify by name a discrete grammatical, syntactic, or orthographic entity and notice when that entity has been somehow besmirched."**

Another reason to love the CMOS folks.

It really is OK for us "to boldly go where no one has gone before."

And other places.

** http://www.chicagomanualofstyle.org/qanda/data/faq/topics/SplitInfinitives .html

MENTOR VS. EDITOR

Mentoring is a brain to pick, an ear to listen, and a push in the right direction.

John C. Crosby

S o...do you look at fiction in a different way when acquiring it for a publisher than when you're reading for pleasure?" This question lands in my lap a lot. And with most questions about publishing, the answer is a definitive "Yes...and no."

Just as I do as a reader, when I read manuscripts for acquisition, I focus on what makes a great story. That's overlaid, however, with considerations specific to my publishing house:

- what slots we have open;
- what genres we buy (and don't);
- previous books by the author and sales figures;
- platform and social media presence;
- manuscript status; and
- professional focus (which differs from platform and is based on the author's focus on writing as a career option).

All of those considerations could affect whether the manuscript is purchased. None deal with the quality of the work—which must come first, before any of those concerns even come into play. But they make a difference about whether I keep reading a proposal or stop and move on to the next one.

When I'm acting as a mentor, those considerations slip away somewhat, and I can focus more on whether or not a book is a great story expertly told. Yet as I advise authors, I will still have in the back of my mind anything that could cause them to stumble on the way to publication. I don't burden the manuscript with thoughts about platform, slot availability, and manuscript status, but I may ask questions such as:

- Who's your dream publisher?
- Do you know if they take this genre?
- What are you doing to make yourself attractive as an author?
- Are you reading the books they publish in your genre?

These aren't personal questions or criticisms of where an author is on the journey. It's a reminder that we are artists in a business. So as a mentor I look at three main areas when working with an author:

> **STORY.** Does it have a sound premise and plotline? Are the conflicts reasonable and completely fleshed out? What's the balance of telling vs. showing? Are characters revealed in dialogue? Does it fulfill genre expectations? (This would take the bulk of time in a mentoring session.)

PRESENTATION. Does it meet the dream publisher's expectations? (In this we look at things like openings, world building, etc.) Is it ready to submit? Are you ready to take on the responsibilities of a published author? What do you need to do to prepare the proposal?

CAREER. Is this a one-off book, or are there dozens of ideas spiraling around in your head, waiting to be told? What do you want your writing career to look like? Who are your favorite authors? Have you examined what they do to build relationships with their fans?

As a mentor, my goal is not only to examine your manuscript to offer up advice and editorial suggestions. Yes, I want to help you become a better writer, but there's more. I want to be that mentor who pushes in the right direction, who is focused on you as a *writer*—not just the author of the one book in front of me.

All writers have a calling—writing is too hard to take it on as a casual hobby—but Christian writers also have an accountability to God and their own beliefs as well as their readers. They have a responsibility to the Giver of their gift and have a charge with upholding a standard. And that leads to the ultimate difference between editor and mentor. As an editor, my primary focus is on the manuscript.

As a mentor, my focus is on the writer—the *person* in front of me, the believer, and the child of God. The goal is a better book, yes, but also to help prepare a writer for the task they've taken on, which reaches far beyond the words on the page.

Comments, Insertions, and Deletions

There's a great power in words, if you don't hitch too many of them together.

Josh Billings

"You want me to use what? But I don't know how to do that! Seriously?"

INSERT: *shot of humble acquisition editor wincing and biting tongue.*

OK, you can stop reading now if you are a whiz at Word's lovely Track Changes feature.

If you're not...well...why not? Why are you ignoring the one tool that most publishers use in their initial edit of a manuscript, the one thing you can say "yes!" to that will make you every editor's friend?

In other words, why are you shooting your career in the foot?

Like shooting yourself in the foot, being unfamiliar with Track Changes won't stop you, but it'll make the next steps increasingly difficult. You can still get published, but you'll limp through the editorial process with any company that depends on it, slowing things down and annoying people who have to pamper you, just because you've not bothered to learn an essential tool of your trade.

Of your JOB.

If you have a day job of any profession, imagine what would happen if you said to your boss, "I don't want to do that because I don't know how. It's too hard to learn."

If this is a regular job, we all know what happens next. But let's pretend it's a contract job. Paperwork has been signed, money paid. The boss is now stuck with you for six months but still has to get the job done. So...he or she either does it themselves (*my* time and scheduling) or hires someone else to do it (*my* budget).

Imagine now how this boss is going to feel about you.

Before you protest that writing isn't your job...I know that it may not be your "day job," the one that keeps the bank and grocery store happy. But if you don't approach it with the same intensity of a job, with the same care about craft and tools, then publishing for you will be a fluke. A short-lived fluke.

Even hobbyists like radio airplane builders or cross-stitchers care that they're doing as much as they can to be the best they can.

Yes, a few publishers don't use Track Changes. Some use pdfs in their editorial process, which is a whole 'nother ball of wax.

Contracts and proofs will come via pdfs. But manuscripts are primarily sent back and forth via email with Track Changes marking the edits. It's fast, easy, and—believe it or not—material is less likely to be lost.

Learning to use Track Changes is incredibly simple. Just pick a document, save a copy, go to the Tools drop-down menu and turn on Track Changes. Then play for ten or fifteen minutes. Insert, add comments, delete. Get familiar with the way an edited manuscript looks.

There are also tutorials online: find them; use them.

There is an old actor's adage that says, if a director asks you if you can ride a horse, say, "Yes! Of course!" Then go learn to ride a horse.

So if an editor asks, "Are you comfortable with Track Changes?"

Say yes.

And don't think you can be sneaky by accepting the changes your editor sends and returning a clean copy. *Ha!* you think. *Now they won't know what I added.*

Oh, yes, we will. That's what the Compare-and-Merge command is for...not that you'd want to learn *that* or anything.

But...keep reading.

TOOLS OF THE TRADE

We are all apprentices in a craft where no one ever becomes a master.

Ernest Hemingway

I get it. Trust me, I do. Patience may be a virtue, but it's not a gift many of us have been blessed with. I know I'm one of the most impatient people in the world. I want what I want RIGHT NOW. I don't know if it's cultural or simply ego, but impatience can plague the best of us.

I know my writing career was probably delayed about a decade because of it.

So I beg all of you not to fall into that trap.

I really get it. I do. We have stories to tell. Important messages. And we want to share them with the world. NOW! We don't want to take the time to do what instructors at conferences call "the essentials." Seriously, in an era of self-publishing, why wait?

The biggest reason: because you can kill your career before it starts.

No, wait . . . don't heckle me just yet. Yes, that's a dire statement. But there's something you need to imprint on your brain right now. Two somethings, actually.

1. You are a better writer than you imagine; you are also a far worse writer than you imagine.

2. Writing is a solitary activity; publishing is a community effort.

This has been true for generations, and remains true today, even in a time when we can type, "The End," and have the book for sale on Amazon that afternoon. And part of working in a community is understanding the expectations of readers and publishers alike. That means research, accepting the advice and guidance of others, and learning the tools of the trade.

The first one? **Microsoft Word.**

Like it or not, this is one of the key tools of the writing craft. Even with all the new programs and platforms that help you plot, Word is the workhorse program for almost all publishers, even the ones that are Mac based. Here are a few tips, which will help your relationships with publishers, beta readers, freelance editors, etc.

1. **Go beyond the basics.** Almost anyone can open Word and start typing. Take the next step and learn how to insert page breaks, set margins, chose fonts. DO NOT DEPEND ON WORD DEFAULTS.

2. **Learn how to use the Track Changes feature.** This is especially essential for many publishers—and most freelance editors—these days. Although some will send edits in pdfs, most still conduct at least the first round of content edits in

Track Changes. If you do not know how to use this feature, you put yourself at a disadvantage with an editor. While a few will work with you in another way, some simply won't. If you don't know how to use Track Changes, they'll tell you to either learn it or give up having any control over the edits in your work. You do not want that.

3. **Keep formatting simple.** Don't try to make your manuscript stand out with all the great layout functions within Word. Most of these won't transfer to a layout program like InDesign, and they have to be stripped out anyway. Your job is to write. Leave the page design to someone else. Use the same font and type size throughout. If you plan to include graphs and charts, it's usually OK to embed them in a proposal, but be aware that they'll need to eventually be submitted as separate, high resolution files.

4. **Use the spelling and grammar checks.** Yes, I know it's tedious and makes you crazy. But it'll also slow you down so you can see your work on an intimate level.

5. **If you have questions, seek out tutorials or coaching.** Tutorials for Word are everywhere, but your best option for help is probably sitting next to you in a workshop at Blue Ridge—a fellow author. Don't be afraid to ask for help. This is yet another reason writers conferences are essential to authors today.

If you plan to self-publish, PLEASE seek out a freelance editor or copyeditor to help you. We are ALL our own worst proofreaders because our brain knows what's supposed to be on the page. So we'll read right over crucial errors.

Take your time. Perfect your manuscript to the best of your ability and use all the resources available to you. In the long run, the patience will be worth it.

"COMMA, COMMA, COMMA, COMMA, COMMA CHAMELEON..."

The song is about the terrible fear of alienation that people have, the fear of standing up for one thing.

Boy George
(aka George Alan O'Dowd)

S orry, having a bit of an '80s flashback there. And fully revealing myself as a grammar dork (as if you didn't already know). I thought dear Boy George was singing about commas until I got my first glance at the song title.

But you can't blame me for the flashback. I recently spent an inordinate amount of time putting commas into a manuscript. And I'm not exactly thrilled about it. Yes, I should leave this to the copyeditors, and probably will in the future. I did force myself to stop a few chapters into the book. But the truth is that I'm an editor by inclination as well as by trade, and, as H. G. Wells said,

"No passion in the world, no love or hate, is equal to the passion to alter someone else's draft."

Preach it, Brother Herbert.

As a writer, I know how hard it is to turn off the internal editor, that whispery voice that clears its throat every time you type a mistake. But to finish your book, you have to. You must! Otherwise, you'll waste a lot of time going over and over and over the same passage, fretting over each word, each comma, each apostrophe.

Likewise, when I evaluate a book for content and structure, I have to put the grammar nerd in the closet. If I don't, I can't see the character arcs for the commas. And, normally, putting aside the virtual red pen is easier than you might think for someone who's been correcting other people's grammar since 1972. (I was just a baby then, I promise.)

But grammar pet peeves live deep inside almost all of us who make a living with language, and those pet peeves will frustrate your editor and bring that virtual red pen roaring from its cave. And they leave an indelible impression. I still remember the last writer who continually used "over" instead of "more than," and I viewed all her submissions askance, as though waiting for her to mess up. Now, of course, the AP style guide has changed their minds on this...

Don't believe me? When I googled "grammatical pet peeves," I got more than a million hits hits. Yep, that's a million red pens waiting to nip it in the bud.

So how do you avoid inadvertently tripping over your editor's pet peeve?

- Read grammar blogs and websites on a regular basis. There are several good ones, and they aren't as boring as they may sound. This is part of learning your craft. Some of them do annual pet peeve lists that can also be helpful and reflect the changing nature of our language.

- After you finish your first draft, go back and review for grammatical gaffes. If you aren't comfortable with doing it yourself, find a friend or critique partner who is.

- Run spelling and grammar check. While spell-checking programs are notoriously unreliable for some things, running the check (as opposed to relying on the squiggly lines or autocorrect) will make the program *highlight* passages for you to think about.

- Set the manuscript aside for a few weeks and read it with fresher eyes. You'll see things in your work you've never seen before.

Remember: grammatical mistakes will not keep you from getting published, but they will get you rejected. While this may sound contradictory, it's based on truth. If you have a fabulous story, most editors can read over a *few* grammatical mistakes. But if they're too numerous, you hit an editor's pet peeve, or if your story isn't strong enough to overcome them, you're toast. I've known more than a few manuscripts that hit the return stack because the errors were so distracting the editor couldn't get past them to the story.

On the other hand, if your manuscript is spot perfect and your story is strong, then you may go on to the next level. Editors love working with midlist authors who are professional enough to have a polished manuscript that's easy to read without the distraction of the red pen popping up every few minutes.

To bring this full circle, I wrote a note to the production editor—who oversees the other editorial stages—to put a high alert on the comma problem with the manuscript, and I stopped reading. After all, I like this author...and I don't want to hear Boy George in my head the next time we have a chat.

Rules? We Don't Need No Stinkin' Rules!

Gather the ingredients, then mix them together and let them merge and disappear into each other, forming something new and unique as you let the context determine the structure of the specific story you're telling.

Steven James, *Story Trumps Structure*

When I was writing columns for *Christian Fiction Online Magazine*, I received this question from award-winning novelist Eva Marie Everson:

What Is More Important: Story or Getting All the Rules Right?

As an editor, I'm tempted to answer her question with one word: **both**. Story *and* the rules are both important. I chose her question, however, because of the underlying thought in it—*What rules are we supposed to follow?*—and the stumbling blocks I see writers trip over all the time that aren't exactly "rules" but some editor's opinion of what the rules should be. It's these opinions that can make success as a writer a moving target.

What Cannot Be Ignored?

- *The craft*: The strength of a story can sometimes trump the flaws of an unpolished manuscript. But rarely, and that goes to the heart of the craft. For the most part, a writer can't ignore appropriate grammar, well-developed characters, and a tightly paced plot. Developing a unique voice fits in there as well, as that becomes a writer's "brand," the one thing above all others that readers will fall in love with and crave in the future. These are all essential.

- *The tension*: All the most compelling stories run on one premise: what went wrong? Everything else derives from that question. If nothing goes wrong, there's no story, just a series of events going nowhere. This may be the biggest mistake new writers make.

So Where Can the "Rules" Be Varied?

One caveat on this: Drift from the rules at your own peril. Editors and readers alike rely on them, and straying from them is the fastest way to get rejected. I always advise new writers to stick to them until they are an established and recognized voice with a house or a particular editor. Having an ally can be essential support as you take something new to the market.

Where Can You Change Your Game?

- *The structure*: I am a serious advocate of the three-act structure for genre novels. It's a storytelling style we are comfortable with in the western hemisphere, and it's been with us for thousands of years. Look up "Welsh triads," and you'll discover that even the ancient bards knew our

brains are wired for loops of three. But some stories just don't lend themselves to it. They need four or five acts, plus a prologue and epilogue. Some genres (such as women's fiction) have a bit more flexibility, but since many editors are trained to look for this, your story should be a seriously compelling one to overcome objections in this area. Sometimes you just need to let the story you want to tell decide what kind of structure the plot has. Good news for those who write organically.

- *Genre requirements:* These may feel as though they're set in stone, but trends change. While romantic suspense, for instance, is supposed to be fifty-fifty hero/heroine viewpoint in a fifty-fifty romance/suspense plot with the couple solving the mystery together, some publishers are beginning to allow some leeway. The bestselling authors in a genre will drive changes, so watch what the favorite authors in your genre are doing.

- *Word length:* Again, hard-and-fast guidelines in this area are changing. Readers are beginning to demand both *longer* books and *shorter* stories. While this sounds contradictory, it's borne out of the new and changing formats available. Readers enjoy flash fiction for their lunchtime or break reads, while still craving expansive tomes to sink into and savor for the next few days. Publishers seem to be looking for epic adventures as well as novellas. Don't be afraid to try something new.

The English language is a living thing that grows and changes. Likewise, the ways we use it to tell stories changes. From the time bards sat around fires with harps and epic tales, the ways we

engage our readers have shifted and flowed. I advise every writer to learn as much as possible about craft, about genre, about all the bothersome rules as possible. Practice them until they make your brain ache.

Some writers flourish under the guidelines, and working through a three-act structure gives their stories wings.

But some do not. And if, after learning the rules, you are one who feels driven to push beyond them, go for it, with the possible consequences in mind. Who knows? Your beyond-the-edge story may be just what an editor is looking for.

Three things not easily restrained:
the flow of a torrent,
the flight of an arrow,
and the tongue of a fool.

Welsh Triad

Turning Your "Idea Factory" into a Writing Career

I don't need an alarm clock. My ideas wake me.

Ray Bradbury, *Writer's Digest*

This morning, I had a new idea for a book. I scribbled down the fifty-word pitch for it, then went back to work. Yesterday afternoon, same thing.

Like most writers, my mind doesn't operate like those of other folks. When a friend and I found a pair of little girl's sandals on a stream bank, she said, "Oh, look. Someone lost her shoes."

I said, "Oh, look. Evidence of a kidnapping."

Why, yes, she did look at me as though I'd grown a second head. Why do you ask?

As most of us know, coming up with a good idea is the easy part. In fact, I can get an idea for a new novel by walking around the parking lot at the grocery store. The numbers go up if I read

bumper stickers and peer into backseats. Good ideas bounce around in my head like ping-pong balls on a daily basis.

But how do you turn all those wild and crazy ideas into a writing *career*? That's the hard part.

Find Your Best Voice

Because of my background, I can write in a lot of different voices. I've studied and loved most genres. Each has its own tone and structure. My own personal "voice," the one I use to interact with friends and family, is a cross between lightly serious and snark. Anyone who's heard me speak (or follows me on social media) knows that as passionate as I am about craft and professionalism, I don't take myself seriously. Life is too short not to laugh a lot along the way.

Thus my best writing voice has a lightly serious tone. Too serious for romantic comedy; too light for most women's fiction and mysteries. Best for suspense, science fiction, and some mainstream.

Find Your Best Brand

After trying to sell more than 350 short stories, I finally got the message that science fiction isn't my forte, no matter how much I love it. Mainstream fiction is the hardest field to break into and the hardest to brand. I couldn't seem to sustain the plot of a straight romance because, well, dead bodies keep showing up.

In fact, every time I get another plethora of ideas, dead bodies appear...in barns, cars, houses, creeks. Even when I attempted a mainstream book, it usually started with a demise of some kind.

I love great villains, too, the kind that make you cringe if you turn out the lights while reading.

So...suspense. Or a romance with dead bodies. Ah, she said, the light dawning: romantic suspense. Small-town crime. Snarky characters who take their work seriously.

I can relate.

Find the Reader's Expectations

Once I had my voice and my brand, I turned outward, toward editors and readers. Who buys romantic suspense and small-town stories? Who reads it? What do they want from it?

Ever wonder if Karen Kingsbury once wanted to be the next Tom Clancy? What if Jan Karon's fans picked up her latest and found that it was a rip-roaring suspense tale set on a cruise ship and in downtown Miami? I suspect she'd find herself faced with many miffed fans.

The writer/reader relationship is an incredibly powerful one, and if you decide to write in a particular genre, then you need to remember what the readers want as well as following the story in your heart. They'll be there for you if you do, every single time.

The Story of Your Heart

Does this go against the sage advice of "write what's in your heart, then find a place for it" and "don't write to the market"?

Not really.

You see, the story in your heart drives your voice, and your voice will show you the brand and the market...the path to your reader.

The rest is the nuts and bolts of craft, of polish, of pushing your heart song to the next level: publication.

To be a successful writer, heart art must blend with business craft. When these two blend smoothly, your words can reach the world.

THE BEAUTY OF EFFICIENCY

Always be a poet, even in prose.

Charles Baudelaire

The heat index today is 105 degrees. The barometric pressure is 29.87 and falling, with 51 percent humidity. It truly is going to be a dark and stormy night.

All of which makes me think of John Sebastian. (Stay with me, this really is going somewhere.)

Back in the day, I had a major crush on John. Even if you don't recognize his name, you probably would his songs. Either as a solo act or in his band (The Lovin' Spoonful), John penned and recorded some of the top songs of the '60s and '70s, as well as one well-known theme for a hit comedy: "Welcome Back," from "Welcome Back, Kotter." He's one of the few people who could play an autoharp on a top-ten Billboard hit ("Do You Believe in Magic?").

John was a master at efficient word play, painting pictures in a concise way that dripped with imagery. Like all great poets, he could lead you on an adventure with just 300 words.

As writers, we can learn a lot from poets, flash fiction authors, and lyricists. Take time to study how they use phrasing and rhythm to help build their images. How varied sentence length can drive or stop movement in a paragraph. After all, writing is more than stringing words together; it's about weaving a tapestry that takes a reader on a magic carpet ride (Oh, look, another '60s song reference!).

I highly recommend that all writers use short passages as a training tool for your craft. Fiction folk should tackle flash fiction. Challenge yourself to build image, character, and plot in five hundred words or less. For nonfiction writers, study devotions. The concise nature of that craft will build writing muscles like you didn't know you had.

And we should all embrace poetry and lyrics. Listen and learn.

Remember that heat index I mentioned at the start of this chapter. Listen to the opening of this song and follow the tone change between the verses and the chorus, from driving to soothing. In just a few words, John makes me feel the heat of the concrete, the relentless heat of a sun so bright there are no shadows, and the sudden relief of night. https://youtu.be/rts7Qdew3HE

Learn the efficiency of a stellar poet, and your prose will sing like no other.

WHAT'S YOUR POINT?

There is only one way to make money at writing, and that is to marry a publisher's daughter.

George Orwell

How long does it take to type a novel?

Not *write*. Not create. *Type*.

I have a friend who can type somewhere between 75 and 80 words per minute. On my best day as a secretary, I could do about 60 or so wpm. I've always been better on a computer than a typewriter (most folks are), so I could, theoretically, type 3,600 words an hour. And as a transcriptionist, I probably could.

As a writer...well, we all know that's a different story. In my writing career so far, my best time was about 2,000 words an hour.

For one hour.

But let's play with the math just a moment, taking out any needed "creative lags." If I can type 2,000 words an hour, then a 100,000-word manuscript would take me fifty hours to type. So if you take

out all those pauses to think, all those moments of editing the last paragraph you wrote, all those stops and starts to allow for plot holes and painted corners and "what color were her eyes?" searches, it would take about fifty hours to type out a novel. About a week's work.

If you received a $5,000 advance for that novel, you'd have made approximately $100 per hour. That's not a bad rate of pay...

Oh, what? I see you have an "aneurysm face" there? What's that you sputter?

Excuse me while I get a towel.

OK, where were we?...ah, yes. Typing is not writing, you sputtered, wetly, in protest.

No, of course not. *All those creative lags are part of the process* and must be figured in. So how long does it take you to finish a book? Say you write one in three months, and you receive a $20,000 advance. That's still more than $40 an hour. A $5,000 advance would be around $10 per hour. (Most typists make more.)

But...you insist...you need at least a year to write a great novel.

Ah. Well, now you see why most authors don't make money at writing. But you knew that. So what's my point?

What's your goal in all this? Why do you write?

There are a lot of folks out there, including some authors, who think that being a writer is "easy money." While most of us laugh at the thought, we still cling to the idea of the best-seller, that breakthrough book that will let us quit the day job, without really examining what it is we want out of a writing career.

I often ask folks at conferences, **"What do you want to get out of a writing career?"** I always get a variety of answers: Money! A contract! Fame! Recognition of talents and gifts. Some write in answer to their calling from God. Others have a message to share.

To be honest, from this editor's point of view, there's no wrong answer to the question. But you do need to answer it. The answer will help you set your goals, your writing schedule, and your deadlines. Don't wait for a publisher to set a deadline. Set it yourself, and stick to it.

If, for instance, you want to make money (George Orwell notwithstanding), the easiest way is to become prolific. Make up your mind that you **are** going to write a novel every three or four months. Do it whether or not they sell. When they do, you'll find you'll sell more often, and once you get five or six novels in print, your royalty statements may start showing a long-term profit. If you're only going to write one or two a year, then you need to give up the idea that you're in it for the money (or pray for a bestseller).

If you have other goals, then define them clearly and draw a path to get there. God gave you a gift. Decide what you're going to do with it. And make it a priority.

Otherwise, you're just typing.

BASICALLY...

Each movement is only learned after you've perfected the one before it.

Scott Hamilton

Ever had one of those "Well, *duh!*" moments in life? One of those times when you realize you've been ignoring the obvious?

I had such a moment when I read Scott Hamilton's *The Great Eight* a few years ago. When he was learning to skate, Scott's hardest challenge was a basic figure eight. What nine-year-old kid wants to do the same *boring* skill over and over? Tracing the same double-circles on the ice, keeping the blade in the same track, hour after hour, day after day? He'd break out, zipping back and forth, doing the stunts that he loved and which seemed to come naturally to him.

Pause. If you don't know who Scott is or have never seen him skate, do yourself a favor and load a few videos of his routines from YouTube. They are a joy. Two of my personal favorites are

his routines to "In the Mood" and "Double Bogey Blues." And knowing his personal story makes some of those routines even more incredible.

OK, end of rabbit trail, back on topic. Scott's coaches refused to let him spend time on the acrobatics he loved until he'd mastered those figure eights. Slowly, he began to realize how important they were. My "duh!" moment came with this paragraph: "As I practiced every day with repetition and consistency, I was building all the small muscles that gave me the ability to control my movements. *I was mastering the fundamentals*" (italics mine). And when he'd mastered the "great eight," he began to win awards.

As a writer, as an editor, as a reader, I *love* great stories. I adore the flashy stuff, the backflips and spins. Most readers do. Editors, in particular, find them beautiful and acquirable.

The problem is too many writers want to do a backflip with a great story without learning the basics. As an editor, I see it every day.

Great concept! Flashy ideas!

Rotten execution!

And the story gets rejected because the fundamentals just aren't there.

Anyone who's sat with me through a pitch session has probably heard this: "I like your idea, but I'll need to see the first three chapters. It's all in the execution."

Here are some of the fundamentals I look for in a manuscript:

- **A great opening page.** This can be achieved in several ways, primarily through action and dialogue. If you plan to open with an internal reflection or a delivery of setting, it needs unique word choices and well-crafted syntax that are better constructed than the Golden Gate Bridge.

- **Dialogue.** Conversations can save or kill a book. One clue is that dialogue needs to sound like we think we talk—not the way we actually do. And every spoken word needs to advance the scene and the plot.

- **Grammar and syntax that sparkle.** For some reason, fiction writers often think that because they can get away with iffy grammar in dialogue, it'll be OK in narrative. It won't. Get rid of tired adjectives. Vary word choices. Stay in the active voice. This does not mean I love overwritten purple prose; it means I look for writers who are skilled in making even the simplest phrase shine.

- **A working knowledge of your genre.** This gets more manuscripts kicked to the curb than almost anything on this list. *Every* genre has reader expectations, whether it's romance, romantic suspense, fantasy, etc. If you are writing Amish romance, then you need to know what the expectations of that genre are. You can learn a great deal by reading your genre and taking notes as well as talking to writers who work in your genre.

- **Likeable, developing main characters that readers will love.** Exceptionally few books can get away with a main character readers don't enjoy spending time with. Flaws are fine; we usually love our friends because of their flaws

as well as in spite of them. But if your character is the kind of person you'd move away from on a bus, look to grow them in different ways. And your main character *does* have to grow and evolve over the course of the novel. One of my favorite quotations about characters is from James Alexander Thom, and it also demonstrates great syntax with simple words: "Whether a character in your novel is full of choler, bile, phlegm, blood, or plain old buffalo chips, the fire of life is in there, too, as long as that character lives."

- **A sharpened plot.** This is why editors want the dreaded synopsis with those sample chapters. An idea that falls flat at the end of the second act or that has an unsatisfying conclusion will make an editor doubt even the snappiest writing.

Yeah, yeah, yeah, some of you are thinking. *We know all of this!*

Do you? Have you polished those fundamentals lately? Because even the most experienced writer can get lazy with the basics. If you haven't sold—or you haven't sold lately—now might be a good time to take a second look.

We all improve the basics (especially me) by studying, reading, and practicing. There are dozens of great writing books out there to absorb. James Scott Bell has an entire library of them. If your plotting is weak, pick up a good screenwriting book like Syd Field's *Screenplay.* Screenwriting books can help with dialogue and so can great movies.

The helps are out there; all you have to do is look. Because the bottom line is, if your fundamentals aren't in place, all the fabulous ideas in the world aren't going to support a writing career.

The Hard Conversations

We may encounter many defeats, but we must not be defeated.

Maya Angelou

Writing is an art. Writing is a craft. Writing is also one of the most personal, self-exposing, nerve-racking things we can do in our lives. We spend hours, days...months pulling back the curtain, showing the Great Oz to the world, whether we write fiction or nonfiction. We expose our minds, our souls, to all comers.

No profession makes us more vulnerable to the world than writing. And few professions include rejection as a regular part of the business. A prolific writer experiences more rejection than anyone but a telemarketer or cold-call seller—and they aren't usually personally invested in their product. Thus, one reason writers often stop short of submitting their work is the fear of rejection.

But, wait, what if they sell? You're over the rejection hurdle, right?

Not exactly. Because for many writers, the rejection of a submission is the *easy* one.

Say what? How is that the easy one?

Because it's not personal. When submissions are rejected by an editor or an agent, it's more than likely because of a market or craft consideration. Craft can be learned. Markets change.

But once you sell, the "rejection"—the changes that an editor requires—becomes a lot more personal. And a much more difficult conversation.

An impersonal rejection stings; an in-depth edit can **sear**.

As I've written about before, editors seldom buy a book because it's perfect. We buy it because we like the author's style or plot or theme. We look for craft. Or talent. Preferably both.

Side note: Talent does not equal sales. Talent is raw potential. Period. It's a lot like inspiration. They both require knowledge, ability to apply that knowledge, and a lot of hard work to make a book that can sell.

But few writers, especially writers that sell on the basis of a pitch or a proposal, walk away without an in-depth edit. One that critiques each detail of your baby, from its wavy hair to its cute toes. While I truly dislike sending out rejections, I despise the editorial letter or the call that must start: "Hi. We need to talk about the changes you need to make."

Authors don't always respond well to these notes and chats. Since I bought their baby, why do I want to change such vital bits? Many reasons, some of which include:

- **Language is not clear**. Yes, it's clear in your head. But not so much on the page to a variety of readers. You're not going to be there to explain it. If it confuses your editor, it's going to confuse some of your readers.

- **The market won't allow it**. The Christian marketplace takes a lot of hits for what it won't allow, but that's true for almost all markets; standards and expectations just differ.
- **You've violated your own rules.** Every book is centered on a "world" of the writer's own design, even if it's a familiar milieu, such as a western. But that world has rules, which involve character development, relationships, geography, plot structure, etc. You can't wander outside those just because you're the author. The reader will feel betrayed. And it's sloppy writing.
- **Your craft slips.** Your genius at deep point of view drops off and you head hop to a secondary character, just because it suits your needs at that moment. *Uh...no.*

Since I'm writer, I've been on the receiving end of this kind of edit. One of my books, *Field of Danger*, looked as though an eighteen-wheeler had run over the manuscript after the first edit. To this day, I still don't like some of the changes. So I know all too well how a heavy edit feels. But at some point, I had to accept that the editor understood her market and her demographic. The book received good reviews and sold as well as my others. Lesson learned.

So what do you do to prevent such an edit?

- **Hire a good content editor.** One who specializes in fiction, preferably your genre. If you don't have the funds to do that, get into a critique group. Bottom line: get some skilled feedback before you submit.
- **Don't submit too quickly.** Finish, take a deep breath, let it sit for a few days. Then read through again. Some authors

I know even read the final draft backwards, which is an old proofreading technique.

And if you do get such an edit, one that smashes your heart?

- **Scream.** Seriously. Find a secluded space and let the rage fly. Trust me; it'll help.
- **Vent.** To your agent, to your spouse, to your friends. Not, however, to your editor. Not yet.
- **Breathe.** After you vent, take a few deep breaths and a long break from the edit. Don't even think about diving into it while you're still upset.
- **Rest. Pray.**
- **Understand.** The editor does not make suggestions or changes arbitrarily. A good editor has sound reasons behind each suggestion. If you don't understand them (or if they're not adequately explained), ask.
- **Slow down.** Go through the changes carefully, but don't change anything on the first pass. Let them ferment.
- **Explain.** If you want to stet something, or leave the original text, explain it. Don't just ignore it. Authors who ignore changes and suggestions wind up being fussed about over coffee. (Yes, we talk about you...)

A good editor is your partner in this. No matter how painful the edit, she's not the enemy out to destroy your hard work. Involve her in your progress; get to know her thoughts on the changes.

Just remember, you both have the same goal: the best possible book for your readers.

A Teacup of Talent

If there is no wind, row.

Latin Proverb

A few years ago, I fell prey to that giant of writer procrastination: **inspiration**. I was *inspired* to write in a genre that I don't particularly read or care for. The stories that struck both brain and heart had a family basis, and I let my knowledge about what I *should* be doing to build a career go dangerously off track. I took a direction my agent suggested would be unwise, but I didn't listen.

Throw into the mix that I had a few "life happenings" that effectively destroyed my remaining creative spirit with mental and physical exhaustion, and you have a recipe for a writing career on its last legs.

Seriously. I almost quit writing entirely. *Eighteen months* of wasted work and life upsets left me weary of continuing the struggle. This wasn't the first time. After my divorce, life became unbelievably hectic and exhausting. For *seven years*, I didn't get a sentence

completed. Forget words; I was lucky I had two brain cells to rub together.

It happens to most of us, sooner or later. With me, the inability to write also came with depression and a bottomed out self-esteem. When I don't—or can't—write, I become someone I don't particular care to be around. Fortunately, I have patient friends.

Inspiration—that beloved "muse" that some many folks believe you need to be a great writer—is a liar and a trap. It can be rare and fleeting, and it's exceptionally deceptive. Somewhere along the way, the "myth" has been born that writers can't work without it.

Wrong. Writers don't need inspiration, although it's nice if it pops along on occasion. What writers need is creativity, discipline...and a cup or two of talent.

So how do you keep going when the ideas dry up and exhaustion turns your creativity into dust?

- **Don't let your "writer brain" control you.** Your writer brain is vital; it makes you who you are. It's the source of your drive to scribble, the database of your skills, and your repository of ideas. It can also be your worst enemy, whispering that you're a failure, that your writing stinks, that you need to be doing something else, that you'll never succeed at this, that you're useless without great ideas and inspiration. Tell that part of it to shut up; you got this. Why?

- **Because you've developed a disciplined plan to write.** When inspiration fails and the ideas turn lame, keep writing anyway. Every day. Journal, write letters (to yourself if

all others have been written). Write nonsense. Doggerels. Whatever. It's all writing; it will all keep you in practice.

- **When ideas fail, plot. PLOT.** Draw a right-angle triangle with the bottom point to the left. Put an inciting incident there and blow something up at the top, and start filling in possible events in between. Will this become a book? Probably not. Maybe so. The point is to work your writer brain and to put stuff down.

- **Make up people.** Do character sketches. Create great heroes and sneaky villains. Give them characteristics like the folks in the mall or at work. Toss them into your fake plot.

These exercises keep the writer brain working and in good shape. Some stuff you may save; the rest you toss. You can always fix what's wrong and polish what's right.

Bottom line: You cannot *fix* a blank page. You cannot *fix* nothing.

Focus on what you do best, not on what you want to do. If you're a writer trying to build a career, you need to focus on one thing. While most writers want to bounce around between genres, most can*not* build a career that way. Save it for later, when you're a famous suspense writer or a great historical romance novelist. Your writer brain will sometimes praise you for anything you write—and you may be good at a lot of things—but seldom are a "lot of things" good for your career.

Don't get distracted just because you can. Don't stray from your course just because you can.

I should take my own advice. (I know my agent would be pleased...)

Yes, yes, I know there are exceptions. I know several authors who have made a go of more than one genre. But if you look at their careers, you will usually find a distinct *plan* of how to make that work. And for every one you can show me who did, I'll show you a dozen who failed at it. Either they sidelined their career, or one genre limped along while the other one galloped.

For most of us, however, distraction and lack of focus are greater enemies than any other obstacles in our writing career.

So take your discipline, focus...and your cuppa talent, and get to work.

A UNIQUE...SURPRISE

It ain't whatcha write, it's the way atcha write it.

Jack Kerouac, *Writer's Digest*

When asked what they look for in a manuscript, editors often answer, "A unique voice," a frustrating answer to any writer. "A unique voice" is hard to define, hard to develop, hard to spot. It borders on trying to define what you like about a particular painting or why you prefer Mozart over Beethoven.

After almost forty years in the business, I also find myself looking for the manuscript that is not just a unique voice but one that *surprises* me. It's the surprises—in voice, quality of work, and plot twists—that make the difference between a good manuscript and a great one.

As an in-house editor, I receive at least ten times as many submissions as I need to fill a list. Competition for a slot is always stiff, and I read a lot of submissions that are good, that will work in the market, and that have a unique voice. But what makes a manuscript truly shine falls into one of three main categories:

- A distinct approach to a common theme, giving the book an exceptional marketing angle.

- A first page that grabs me by the throat and won't let go. In other words, once I start reading, I can't stop.

- A thorough, professional presentation that includes synopsis, marketing plan, comparative titles, bio, etc., which demonstrates that the author views this as a business as well as storytelling opportunity.

A book that has all three will bounce out of the slush pile as though it were made of helium.

One such novel was written in the women's fiction genre, and it dealt with grief, loss, and alienation from God. Not a unique theme at all. The voice is first person, laced with humor, and a bit snarky. Again, well done, but not unusual. But the title got my attention, the presentation held it, and the first page grabbed me immediately. The manuscript was finished, which meant I didn't have to wonder if the author could successfully complete the story. The result was that I contracted *The Dog That Talked to God* by Jim Kraus faster than I have any other book. It went on to be one of the biggest hits I ever acquired.

But, you may ask, how do you make a book distinctive if you're writing a genre that has stricter guidelines? I have bought a lot of those as well: romantic comedies, romantic suspense, western, and historical romances.

One way to make a genre tale stand out is to create characters who are engaging and likeable. Flawed but strong. Someone the reader will want to be like or be friends with. Because plots can be redirected, historical inaccuracies edited, and grammar

corrected. But if your characters are flat and without merit, no editor in the world will want to spend the time to fix them.

So...surprise an editor with a character they can root for and enjoy spending time with for the next few days, in a story that hasn't really been told before, in a way that is truly your own. Then wait for The Call.

Pursuing a Mulligan

Don't be afraid to start over if something isn't working. It can often be easier and more effective than revising over and over.

Emily Rodmell

A "mulligan," as most golfers will know, is a bit of forgiveness when your shot goes so far afield that no recovery is possible. Instead of trying to shoot the ball from wherever it ended up, you replay the stroke.

Basically...a do-over. Lovely concept and a great generator of hope. The Bible, for instance, is full of folks who got another shot at something, and we are often told that ours is a God of second chances. One of my favorite authors, Allison Bottke, headed up an entire series of books entitled *God Allows U-Turns*. And He does.

But no one, not even God, said those second chances were easy.

A few years ago, I had written myself into a proverbial corner. I had plotted out three books based in a small Tennessee town and centered on three sisters: April, June, and July. (The second child in the family turned out to be a boy; "May" wound up being

"Mark." I suspect that only other writers will understand why I had no control over that...) The first two books had come out (*Field of Danger* and *House of Secrets*), and I was working desperately on the third book. Only...

...my editor hated my plot. Not just an element here or there but the whole thing, from the opening teaser right through to the denouement. It was just not working for her or the line. She rejected the book.

After I stopped gnashing my teeth and tossing furniture around, I pouted. A lot. *She doesn't know what she's talking about. I'm a horrible writer, unable to handle any kind of reasonable plot. Why did God curse me like this!* Yep, and a whole lot of other self-pitying nonsense that's part of the editorial grieving process.

Seriously, getting that kind of editorial news sends most writers careening through several stages of grief, usually in one afternoon: denial, anger, bargaining, depression, and acceptance. New writers tend to take longer to work through them. I'm old, however, and I've been doing this a long time. My process currently lasts about twenty minutes.

Now what? This wasn't a normal rejection (if there is such a thing). I'd spent the previous two books building up the history and character of the third sister. I had a town. I had a police force, including the hero of this book. Did I just drop it and leave all those questions unanswered for the readers? Try something new?

Or...just start over. I shot off a quick email to my editor, asking if the characters were OK. Would she be willing to look at the same

people and setting with a new plot? The answer came back almost immediately.

Sure.

A mulligan. I got a do-over. I took July, who had renamed herself Lindsay (another thing not in my control given the history I'd saddled her with) and her hero Jeff (still a deputy sheriff), and I dropped them into a brand new adventure, one with lots of action, seriously dark twists, and the small-town setting common to the first two. I got to revisit the other two sisters and their now-husbands and answer all the questions left by the other two books. The result—*Memory of Murder*—was my best-selling, best-reviewed novel up to that point.

My Best Advice to Make This Possible: Don't Fall in Love With Your Story

As an editor, I see this problem all the time—and in the terms of building a writing career, it *is* a problem. Writers *must* be passionate about what they do, but sometimes they forget that the passion should be about the *writing*—not any one particular book. God has given you a remarkable *gift* with which you can tell lots of different stories.

If you fall in love, becoming totally committed to one story, one character, then you run the risk of being completely heartbroken when the rejections come (and they always do). You get mired in the tale you're trying to weave, and you become reluctant to even edit, much less rewrite.

Instead, fall in love with your gift. Fall in love with what God's leading you to do. When you finally realize there are literally

hundreds of ways you can use God's gift for His purpose in your life, rejection—or that twenty-five-page editorial letter—becomes just another rock in the path. One to be journeyed around so that the stories can move on. As the old proverb says: "Failure lies not in falling down. Failure lies in not getting up."

Do You Sometimes Wake Up Evil?

Those who prefer their English sloppy have only themselves to thank if the advertisement writer uses his mastery of the vocabulary and syntax to mislead their weak minds.

Dorothy L. Sayers

A friend of mine, Kevin, had applied for a position with a nationally recognized company, and the first interview had gone extremely well. As had the second one with the hiring manager. Kevin became even more excited when they notified him that he was one of the top candidates. He then received an email with instructions to go to a certain clinic for a drug test and a link to a psychological test online.

Kevin thought seriously about handing in a resignation for his current position. But a nagging thought he couldn't quite put into words made him hesitate, and Kevin decided to rely on that instinct that many of us count on to keep us from walking down dark alleys and stepping in front of buses.

Kevin had no worries about the drug test. He hadn't partaken in anything illegal since college—and he was well past college. The psychological test? Well...

Kevin regularly had problems with those. While he was quite sane and exceptionally stable, he was also intelligent, had done a lot of writing for various publications, and seldom saw anything as black/white or yes/no. You could easily say that Kevin saw the world in as many shades of gray as he did hues of the rainbow.

Only...most psych tests are also timed. It does make a difference if you spend an average of five seconds per question, then suddenly hang over one for two minutes. But Kevin wanted this job. So he took a deep breath, registered for the test, and prepared himself to answer more than two hundred questions.

The first part of the test went quite well. Then some of the questions began to repeat themselves, although they were phrased in different ways. This annoyed Kevin, but he kept plugging. As new questions popped up, some seemed intentionally confusing, further dampening his mood. Then, finally, he came to the question that stopped him cold.

DO YOU SOMETIMES WAKE UP EVIL?

He stared at it. It was a yes/no question, with no wiggle room. Yet, Kevin, humorist that he is, had a different first thought, based on an old comic standby.

DO YOU SOMETIMES WAKE UP EVIL?

NOT ALWAYS; SOMETIMES I LET HER SLEEP IN.

He didn't get the job.

Syntax matters.

Sometimes, we get tricked into thinking that it doesn't. There are a dozen or more internet memes making the rounds that replace letters in a paragraph with symbols and numbers, then challenge us to understand them. They praise us as intelligent folks if we can decipher them. This is nonsense. We can read it because the SYNTAX in those paragraphs is well constructed, and anyone with a halfway decent high school education can fill in the blanks.

Then there are the ones which are basically "Yoda-ese." Paragraphs with no misspellings but screwy structure. Can we still understand them? Of course, because the thoughts conveyed are simple and fairly straightforward, as the writers intended them to be. The creators of these memes want them to go viral, not be a Mensa exam.

They may be fun, but don't be fooled.

Instead, talk to a lawyer about why you can't put a comma in a phrase that *The Chicago Manual of Style* demands you must because it would change the legal meaning of the sentence. Talk to a comedian who uses syntax to lead an audience through a series of jokes to a callback that's made even more amusing by the use of clever syntax. Talk to an ad guru or a politician who knows how to spin a "misspoken" sentence a dozen ways to Sunday.

Talk to a Bible translator who has to work with not only Greek, Hebrew, and Aramaic words but also the cultural idioms and syntax unique to those languages.

Precise syntax will make your prose snap and engage the reader in a way that will keep the pages turning. It's a part of the craft that

you need to polish, read aloud, and polish some more. Because bad syntax *can*, in fact, make your reader "see" something you never intended.

Like evil sleeping in the next room.

SEA WALKER, MOUNTAIN MOVER—NOT DEUS EX MACHINA

de·us ex ma·chi·na *noun* \\'dā-əs-'eks-'mä-ki-nə, -'ma-, -,nä; -mə-'shē-nə\ *a character or thing that suddenly enters the story in a novel, play, movie, etc., and solves a problem that had previously seemed impossible to solve.*

Merriam-Webster

I love music. All kinds. I think God put music in our souls to be able to reach out to other people and help us form community, which is a vital part of the human experience. Seldom do I run across a type of music I've not heard, studied, or loved. I still remember when I was introduced to AfroCelt, Brudda Iz, Les Pretres, Tiesto, and The Killers. My favorite flautist remains James Galway, although I'm also fond of medieval recorder tunes. I like Hank Williams, Hank Williams Jr., and Hank III. One of my goals is to own a complete set of the Child ballads (I'm missing volume 2). For years, my friend Sharon and I would take up

residence at the front table in the music room of an Irish pub on Friday nights, waiting to see what the band would deliver. What I listen to on any given day depends on what mood I'm in.

And I'm an unabashed lover of Southern gospel. Like any other type of music, there's good...and not so good. But the message in all of them speaks to my heart. And sometimes the editor in me.

My rental car for the trip to the 2014 Blue Ridge Mountains Christian Writers Conference had satellite radio, so my trip companions were the '60s, '70s, '80s, Sinatra, and Southern gospel. Call it a mood. But as I was maneuvering through the twenty miles or so of curves and tunnels on the border of North Carolina, a song that struck that editorial nerve was the Perrys' version of Kyla Rowland's "This Old Sinner Testifies." The song speaks of what happens when we rely on Christ when we're drowning in life's trials and sorrows. He comes to us, lifting us up out of the waves. This is truth. There is no greater companion in life than the Lord. He redeems and turns around our lives.

So why shouldn't we be allowed to let that happen in our novels, for God to come down like the Greek *deus ex machine* to save the day?

Because while it may be good faith, it's lazy writing. Because there is a major difference in a character who relies on God and one whose character arc is short-circuited by a miracle. Because novels—at their best—are about *people*, not miracles.

Readers want to fall in love. They want to root for the main characters, to cry with them, grow with them, embrace their trials and triumphs. They want to live with these folks awhile and enjoy spending time in their world. Whatever the story is,

however fast-paced the plot, more often than not, it's the *people* that keeps readers turning the page. The greatest plot in the world will not keep readers engaged if they don't care about the outcome for the main characters. And great characters in the hands of a skilled storyteller can overcome some of the worst plot goofs ever published.

Most of us don't live each day by grand miracles dropped on us from out of nowhere. We live by faith, by relying on God for strength, wisdom, inspiration. By persevering because we believe in His guidance and direction. By forming community with other believers, who deliver the smaller "miracles" of unexpected support and encouragement—the friend who shows up with dinner after a hard day or the church that pays an electric bill for an unemployed single dad.

The "miracles" in our lives aren't usually the "moved mountains" of God—it's that Christ's love and sacrifice, His grace and wisdom, allows *us* to move the mountains, to achieve when all is lost, to discover hope within ourselves and our faith in Him.

Now...don't get me wrong. I know all too well that true, inexplicable miracles happen; I've been around for a few. And I'm *not* saying an author should never include one in a book.

What I'm saying is that God should never have to descend from on high to save a hero because the author has written the plot into a corner. Don't call on God to fix a mess because the writing has gone astray.

I frequently speak with authors who want something to happen in their manuscript, who want the main character to do something because the *author* needs it to happen. Not because it makes

sense in the plot or fits the character arc but because the *author* insists it has to happen.

Not going to work. If that event (miracle or not) needs to happen, then it has to be "written to." The character has to develop to a point where it makes sense. The plot has to logically reach that moment; it can't just leap out of the ether like the "god from the machine." Otherwise the author has betrayed the plot, the character...and the reader. An editor will fuss about the first two, but the reader will turn away and never look back.

You don't want that. So stay true to the character and the craft, to the plot as outlined, and—most of all—the desires of your reader. Write the best book that you possibly can without relying on shortcuts—or miracles.

God will take care of the rest.

Love/Hate Spell/Check

I have a spelling checker
It came with my PC
It plainly marks for my revue
Mistakes I cannot sea
I've run this poem threw it
I'm sure your please to no,
It's letter perfect in it's weigh
My checker tolled me sew.

Anonymous

My brother had trouble learning to read. Spelling tests were the source of nightmares. His little sister (me) had issues staying out of trouble when unobserved by an authority figure. My mother resolved this dilemma by sitting on the couch with me on one side, my brother on the other, and a book in her hands.

A belt also rested in her lap, but I don't remember it ever being used. Presence was usually sufficient in those days.

As a result, my brother learned to read. Despite being five years younger, so did I. Throw in third-grade phonics training, and I've been a spelling and grammar nerd ever since. Two of my favorite classes in college were History of the English Language and Advanced Grammar. And when I came across this quotation from Mark Twain's autobiography, I knew there were others out there who loved all the vagaries of the English language as much as I did.

> Ours is a mongrel language which started with a child's vocabulary of three hundred words, and now consists of two hundred and twenty-five thousand; the whole lot, with the exception of the original and legitimate three hundred, borrowed, stolen, smouched from every unwatched language under the sun, the spelling of each individual word of the lot locating the source of the theft and preserving the memory of the revered crime.

I am a self-confessed "word nerd," and, like most writers, I've had a long love/hate relationship with computerized spellchecking. As in the poem at the start of the this chapter, some of the elements they miss (or autocorrect) are laughably bad. In a novel, the grammar check is a particularly tedious nag. The program will flag dialogue that's fine and narrative that's perfect. And don't get me started on sentence fragments.

On a first draft, when you're focused on story and plot, you can benefit from turning off or ignoring all the red, green, and blue squiggly lines that show up under text. Just like you should turn off your internal editor, the one that makes you search fifteen

minutes for *the* perfect word, you shouldn't be focused on spelling and grammar in the first draft.

But there are three very good reasons why you *should* run a spelling and grammar check on your novel before you submit it, no matter how mind-numbing or boring it is to spend a couple of hours clicking through every perfectly fine "correction" the program redlines.

- **You are your own worst proofreader.** No one—not you, not me, not Karen Kingsbury—should rely on their own proofing. You *will* read over what really is there, seeing only what you intended to be there. This doesn't make you a bad proofreader; it makes you human.

- **Spelling and grammar checks are tools, not fixes.** They were never intended to make your copy perfect all on their own. But they will find mistakes you didn't realize you made. They will also highlight easily overlooked issues, such as subject/verb agreement, frequently misused structures, and use of the passive voice. And typos. Y'know, those little things that can get you rejected.

- **They highlight sentences for reconsideration.** I run a spell and grammar check on every manuscript before it goes to typesetting, even *after* it's been through a couple of edits and revisions. One reason is because some sentences that show up in the dialogue box look just fine in context, but out of context they appear unbelievably stupid or misguided. These are the kind of sentences that can trip a reader up in a heartbeat. It gives me a chance to reevaluate them, to see if anything could be tweaked for a smoother reading experience.

When I run that little poem up there through a spelling and grammar check, it only finds two mistakes, but it highlights the entire sentence, giving me one more chance at getting it right. The rest is up to me. For instance, when I ran this article through the check, it flagged a sentence as possibly having a subject/verb problem. The sentence was correct, but it made me look at it twice, and I ended up rewriting it.

Writing is hard enough without ignoring a tool that can help. Even one that occasionally makes us laugh.

Using Body Language to Develop Character

Body language can reveal more about character than almost any other detail.

Annie Weatherwax

Lying, out-and-out tall tales, deceptions, and dark secrets. These form the center of many novels. They create tension, conflict, and suspense. But how does an author let the reader, as well as other characters, know that a lie has been cast without writing on the page, "He's lying," or, "Jane knew he lied." After all, *how* did Jane know he lied?

Was it the tilt of his head, the lack of eye contact? Did he cover his mouth with one hand or rub the side of his nose? Was he focused on an object to his left and below shoulder level? Did he smile at the wrong time in a sentence or become defensive when questioned? All of these actions can reveal deception of some kind, and savvy readers will recognize this immediately, without being told.

Body language is one of the best tools adept authors have. It can speed dialogue along or can be used for appropriate beats, allowing the reader to catch up and have an insight into the characters. Writers use body language to convey mood, temperament, and—in some cases—even upbringing. A popular television show, *Lie to Me*, is based on the science of facial expressions and what they reveal about people. And if you really want a crash course on body language, watch police reality shows like *The First 48*. Police interrogation techniques are geared toward getting people to react, even if they don't speak. Body language reveals more than people want to admit.

One of the best uses of body language is to get rid of dialogue tags. Doing so serves a dual purpose: cleaning up "said" constructions and more accurately revealing character. For example, compare these two:

> "You don't have to do this," Sophie said tensely. "He didn't do anything wrong."
>
> "Yeah, I do," David insisted, spitting on the street. "He's behind all of this, all of the problems you and I have been having."

Or

> Sophie's eye twitched, and she crossed her arms tightly over her chest. "You don't have to do this. He didn't do anything wrong."
>
> David cleared his throat and spit to his left, leaving a brown stain on the sidewalk. He shoved the gun down

in his waistband. "Yeah, I do. And you're wrong. He's behind all of this, all of the problems you and I have been having."

Body language can help you *show*, not *tell*. With "You need to show, not tell" being the most frequent advice given out to new writers, I'm often asked for advice on how to do that. One of the fastest ways to make the transition is to stop using words that *describe* emotions (frightened, depressed, sad, happy, lonely, loving) and translate those into actions. How does someone who's a loving, compassionate person behave toward a sad friend? How does that sad friend respond? What's the difference in physical expressions of "happy," "giddy," or "ecstatic"?

For example, fear is an involuntary response to a threat. Sometimes we immediately go on the defensive—other times, we run. Or freeze. So what do those reactions look like?

> David pulled his gun, waving it wildly. Joe, terrified, couldn't even form words.

Or

> David yanked his gun free, his shaking arms driving the barrel in a dozen directions. Joe's eyes widened, and his jaws opened and closed silently, spittle forming at the corners of his lips. His gut tensed, and a small puddle edged outward from his feet.

Well, some reactions are little more obviously involuntary than others.

Body language can set the tone of a scene and provide an atmosphere in which to immerse the reader. For example:

> Sophie tugged the fedora tighter on her head, turning the brim down as she hunched her shoulders into her trench coat. She braced her shoulder against the icy brick of the alley's entrance, eyes downcast but watchful. She pressed her feet together as she pushed her hands into the pockets, her left one once again gripping the unyielding gun stock in trembling fingers. She took one deep breath, squared her shoulders, and stepped out of the alley, facing David and Joe.

So what's going on here? When most people read this paragraph, they get a sense that it's night, possible raining, without being told either. It's cold, and Sophie is definitely up to something—and we know this without being told specifically.

Learning body language cues is an essential part of an author's craft. If you're uncertain about which body postures and facial expressions indicate confidence, shame, happiness, sadness, love, or deception, do a quick search on the internet. Articles about body language abound, but also look for blogs and sites with a forensics or investigative basis, such as Eyes for Lies (eyesforlies.com).

The more you study people, the better characters you will develop—and the more your writing will grow in its quality and uniqueness.

And, whatever you do, don't mess with your hair when you're pitching a book to an editor or agent (it signals lack of confidence).

A Frenzy over Facts

All history is gossip: the important thing is to know which gossip is history.

Gore Vidal

In the past, I have mentored a number of authors, in addition to those I work with through a publisher. Sometimes new writers just need career direction; other times, we talk about writing or a particular story they're working on. Occasionally, these have become long-term friendships, and to this day, these are authors who call me for counsel...or consolation.

Recently, I had a frantic email from one of these friends, who had gotten her edits on an upcoming historical romance set in the antebellum South. About a particular scene in the book, her editor had written simply: "This needs to be changed. It wouldn't happen like this during this time period."

My friend didn't know what to do. First, the scenario was key to her plot. Second, it was based on a diary from the time period—so she knew that, in actuality, it *would* have happened because it *had* happened.

This isn't the first time I've heard this complaint. Authors of historical books hear it all the time, usually from people who believe they have studied the period thoroughly—or whose knowledge is based on television series or films. Or from reviewers who base their knowledge of a time period on previously published novels. Or from readers who think...

You get my drift.

While historical accuracy is vital, there's a limit, especially when it comes to character behavior. Nonprofessional historical research can take an author only so far. Or a reader. Or any amateur historian. History is too transient and too complex for certainties about human behavior; for every fact we know definitively, there are hundreds that haven't been unearthed. Millions of lives have passed on this planet with little or no record of how they behaved.

I've met a few true experts on history, and most of them don't write or read historical novels, probably with good reason. One professor I knew had spent his entire thirty-year career studying the literature and history of the seventeenth century. When I asked him if a certain scenario could have happened, he just shrugged and said, "Social mores have changed significantly over the ages. Governments, words, and phrases come and go. People...not so much. Since Adam lied to Eve, we've cheated, scammed, loved, hated, deceived, mocked, and bullied each other. War has always made for bitter heroes and wounded warriors. We've lifted up and torn down. It's not so much about what people *could* do. It's about what we *choose* to do. And why."

Scarlett O'Hara scandalized Charleston. Would it have happened the way Margaret Mitchell portrayed? Probably not. Well-born

widows didn't go around behaving like that. But we believe how Scarlett *chose* to behave because of *who* Scarlett is. We believe it because of how Mitchell developed her character before all that happened.

If a heroine faces ruin because of the social mores of the Regency *bon ton*, it's because of the choices she's made and how she lives those out. It's a great set-up for conflict and consequence: ruin or the hero dies. Ruin or her family suffers. Ruin for herself or...whatever. In the hands of a skilled author, this becomes a heart-pounding story that uses historically accurate details about a particular social group as a foundation. Those details need to be as accurate as possible to keep the genre reader engaged.

But for a critic (or a reader) then to say a woman of that status would *never* violate the rules of the *bon ton* means that either the author hasn't done a good job developing the character or that the critic needs to spend a few more hours studying human psychology. After all, one reason people understood the consequences of stepping out of the norm is because others had already done so—and paid the price.

Some critics have complained, for instance, that Diana Gabaldon's Jamie Fraser (*Outlander*) is a man out of his time. He certainly stands out from his peers, who are rather grittily portrayed. But if you read her book closely, you'll discover the reasons Jamie behaves the way he does, including the upbringing that instilled in him beliefs and points of view that vary from men of his time period. Yet, in some choices he makes, Jamie is very much a man of his time, infuriating the heroine, Claire, to no end.

And that Claire is astonished and alarmed at some of his choices brings into focus why so many critics berate historical romances as being inaccurate as to the behavior of main characters. This is a fine line most historical romance authors have to walk...and hate to walk. If most pre-1800 romantic heroes behaved completely true to their time period, most modern women would put a knife in their kidneys before sundown.

They would certainly not enjoy a romance written about them.

Dorothy Dunnett, in her Lymond and Niccolo series, does an amazing job of keeping her characters' behavior mostly true to period. As a result, her books (which are not romances in the modern sense) are engaging, fascinating, and more than occasionally infuriating. Toward the end of one book, the hero makes a choice that is true to the time, the situation, and his character... and I threw the book against a wall. Literally. Dented the drywall. I did *not* want that to happen! I wanted the twentieth-century version! Much blasphemy ensued. Yet, in the end, I loved her all the more for it.

So what's a historical author to do? Should they develop heroes and heroines modern readers can relate to or stay authentic to the period? Either way, it seems, someone will be annoyed. Don't be surprised by this.

First, you're an author. Someone, somewhere, is going to be annoyed. You will not make all readers happy. Fact of life. Accept it. Do not try to change their minds. Move on.

Second, make the "trackable" details as accurate as possible. When your settings, expressions, furnishings, events, politics, fashion, etc., are pitch-perfect, it reveals how much research you

invested in before writing the book. Readers will cut you more slack if you've demonstrated that you really do know and understand the era.

Third, build anachronistic behavior in from the beginning. If your character is going to act "out of time," make it part of the character development, even from childhood, if you have to. For instance, my mother wanted me to be the typical 1950s girl growing up. Dolls, curls, dresses. Instead, I kept dragging home pretty rocks, animal bones, and star maps. My clothes had more red mud than crinolines. Pre-1840 (when the women's movement began), this would have been trampled out of me. But I had a mother who had walked away from her dreams, so she encouraged mine. Eventually, she gave up on crinolines and pin curls.

My point? Don't let a character violate the rules of the *bon ton* easily if she's embraced and loved them all her life. Make her struggle in her own skin. Torture her. Give the reader something to grasp in her character.

Fourth, acknowledge when something is anachronistic. If you know something is going to stand out, write an author's note that covers the how, what, and why, and make it part of your proposal. If you have an "anachronistic" event that's based on a real happening, say so up front.

For instance, Deanne Gist did this in *Maid to Match* when she put a letter in the book that detailed the differences between the late nineteenth-century servant/houseowner relationships in England and those in the American South. Her book, set at Biltmore House in North Carolina, details the very real, completely documented upstairs/downstairs relationship that Mrs. Vanderbilt

had with her servants. Deanne's details were based on historical records, but she knew that the microcosmic social group in North Carolina would annoy readers of British dramas of that time period. Basically, she let folks know that Biltmore House was not Downton Abbey, and the same standards did not apply.

So how did I advise my frantic friend? I told her to email her editor and explain the situation. I suggested that she ask her editor if this was a make-or-break issue, and, if not, for ideas on how to make it work. And offer up that explanation for the reader.

She'll still get letters. But she'll also get new fans.

SEPARATING THE WOMEN FROM THE...OTHER WOMEN

With women's fiction, readers can laugh about serious issues and be assured that others have encountered the same problems and overcome them.

Beth Hill, *The Editor's Blog*

I recently had an author I admire a great deal try her hand at a romance. I was all for it; she has a great voice and has been nominated for a number of awards for her women's fiction.

The manuscript she turned in made me laugh, and it was a lovely story. It was not, however, a romance. Nor was it entirely women's fiction. The macro editor made a number of suggestions to bring it in line with a true romance, but neither the author nor I were thrilled with what it would take. So after a long conversation, we decided the author should shift the book to women's fiction. That's more her brand, and it's a genre she's comfortable with.

This edit took place on a level few authors ever have to deal with, but it reminded me of how often I hear questions from new writers about the differences between women's fiction with romantic elements and a romance.

There are variations on each, but the basics are simple.

- A ROMANCE focuses on the love story. It features a likeable hero and heroine and dual points of view that must have equal weight. BOTH characters must grow (with defined character arcs), changing as they fall in love. The conflict is relationship-based. The obstacles must be real and not something they could clear up with an honest conversation over dinner.

- WOMEN'S FICTION focuses on the heroine's journey, usually through a period of trial or significant life change. Ideally it features ONLY her point of view, and she is the one who has the prominent character arc. While there can be a romantic element, that's not the primary point of the novel. The conflict is based on obstacles that prevent her from reaching her emotional/spiritual goal.

Authors sometimes protest that conforming to genre conventions restrict the author's voice. And how such conventions shift frequently. And how every publisher seems to be different.

But remember that genre conventions aren't just publisher requirements; they describe reader expectations as well. A consumer who picks up a book that's described as a mystery expects such a novel to follow expected conventions of the mystery genre. If it doesn't, they *will* let you know.

Readers who love women's fiction know what it is about that genre they adore. Same thing with romance. If your novel doesn't fit within either of these basic formats, then it may be another genre altogether. The best path is to learn the conventions of all genres, including mainstream, and see which comes the closest to fitting your story.

SQUIRREL!

Writing is 3 percent talent and 97 percent not wasting time on the internet. [*]

Anyone who spends more than fifteen minutes in conversation with me realizes focus is not my forte. Getting from point A to point B may take a detour through points K, S, J, and D, depending on the topic. While I've never been diagnosed with an attention deficit, and I resist labeling of most kinds, I've always had issues with distractions.

In part, I think this is because I was born with a writer's brain and infinite curiosity. I want to know about *everything*, as I believe most writers do. When I was a teenager, my friends learned quickly *not* to ask me how to spell a word. While I'd know most of the time, if I had to look up a word, the conversation was pretty much over. A dictionary is a treasure trove of information. Etymology fascinates me, and the definition and derivation of one

[*] I've searched for the source of this floating internet meme but found too many claims to its origin. So I left it anonymous for now. It's funny. And all-too accurate.

word leads to another, which leads to another...and down the rabbit hole I'd go, whatever conversation I was having forgotten.

Speaking of rabbits...I recently got involved in a Facebook conversation about squirrels (wait for it...). It actually started as a comment about marmots (a type of ground squirrel)—specifically about people who eat them. This led to comments about eating other unusual sources of consumable protein, such as venison, rabbit (here it is), possum, and squirrel.

I've eaten squirrel. While it was a long time ago, it's not something you forget easily. I've seen one skinned. Even harder to forget. And while that Facebook chat gave me childhood flashbacks about my grandmother (who fried the squirrel) and my brother (who procured and skinned it), it also made me think of Dug, the dog in the movie *Up*, and his perfect doggy distraction call of "Squirrel!"

So perfect is it as a code word for distraction that my friends and I now use it when we've strayed so far off the original topic of a conversation that we've forgotten where we were going in the first place. They have also gotten accustomed to interrupting one of my stream-of-consciousness flows with the phrase, "bunny trail," which is usually accompanied by a hand signal that bears a great resemblance to Little Bunny Foo Foo hopping through the forest.

This is why I use notes when I speak in public. Not because I'll forget what I want to say but because if I don't, the first time a rabbit trail beckons, I'll be off like Dug after a squirrel. The notes help keep me on point.

Writing can be the same way. The internet can be a horrid source of distractions far beyond Facebook or Twitter or any other social

media. The internet also bristles with information that looks like research. Articles that might contain a smidgen of historical information you might need also contain hyperlinks to other articles of equally fascinating information. You can look up the origin of a phrase from the 1930s and find yourself wandering the Waterloo battlefield an hour later.

In the meantime, your character is waiting patiently for you to finish the conversation.

Beyond your online distractions, the "squirrels" of everyday life beckon. Phone calls. Housework. A day job. Children. Especially children. I don't know many folks who have a lot of free time. Few writers I know have huge blocks of time just waiting to be filled with their glorious wordsmithing. We have to make time to write, squeezing it in between other obligations and desires. Every writer knows how deadly distractions can be to those precious fifteen- or thirty-minute blocks.

But distractions can, in fact, help your writing as well. Sarah Baughman wrote a great blog post[**] on why distractions should be controlled but not eliminated. Distractions—the everyday life around us as well as interminable internet linking—also inform us. They reveal character development, new plot twists, strange motivations for actions.

As a writer friend of mine is prone to say: All of life is novel fodder.

The goal, instead, is to control them, not eliminate them. The best key?

[**] http://writeitsideways.com/distracted-it-could-help-your-writing/ Accessed 1/8/2020.

Take the writing advice of others sparingly. Find what works for you. For instance, some folks recommend having a good desk for writing. I have a nice computer desk, but my feet dangle (yes, I'm short). So after about fifteen minutes, my legs ache. The recliner works best for me, which I discovered when I had a crippling bout of vertigo. It's a small recliner so it encloses and stabilizes me. It puts the screen close, so I'm not distracted by the, yes, squirrels outside the window. And with the screen relatively close, I don't have to move my eyes much.

The vertigo also trained me to write in short spurts. This is a gift to an easily distracted writer.

Some folks need silence in order to focus. Others need a coffee shop so they have something to shut out. For me, a restaurant is too distracting, whereas silence allows my mind to wander. Classical music or soundtracks help me shut out other distractions. Except for flute music. I play the flute, and those give me performance flashbacks. And not vocals because I start to sing along.

Some folks write on a treadmill. I discovered the hard way that this makes me motion sick.

I don't have to worry about family interruptions, but I've had to learn how to ignore the phone. A friend has warned her family that when she's writing, interruptions are forbidden unless blood, flood, or fire is involved.

The bottom line is that distractions are inevitable, and they can be helpful. But they must be controlled. And like your voice, the management of your writing time is as unique as you are.

THOSE NASTY FORM REJECTIONS

You must keep sending work out; you must never let a manuscript do nothing but eat its head off in a drawer. You send that work out again and again, while you're working on another one. If you have talent, you will receive some measure of success—but only if you persist.

Isaac Asimov

A few years ago, two of my favorite agent bloggers, Rachelle Gardner and Nathan Bransford, posted about the whys and wherefores of rejection. In the comments that followed, writers expressed quite a bit of frustration about form rejections, those undetailed, "does not fit our line" slips of paper or emails that most writers could paper a house with. Or less savory places.

You know the ones I'm talking about—if you've been writing and submitting for any length of time, you probably have a few lying around...or in a folder on your computer. Those "no thanks" notes that say nothing about your work or the real reason you

were turned down. Is the manuscript really lousy or is my timing off for the industry?

I understand that frustration. In the (many) years between sales, I received a lot of these. So many I stopped counting. I have about 350 paper ones stored in a variety of boxes and enough in files on my computer to clog up a flash drive. Some were mere multiple choice forms than an editor had checked a reason. I got a lot of "doesn't fit" responses. I also received responses that didn't make any sense at all, like the one where a straight science fiction piece was rejected because "we don't accept horror." Mmm...OK.

So why do editors use them? Three reasons:

1. Time
2. Cowardice
3. Perspective

Seriously.

1. **Time.** You probably understand the time thing: Most editors receive more manuscripts than they can possibly use, and they have NO time to send personal responses or explanations why a work is being rejected. But it goes beyond the fact that writing out a critique takes a lot of time.

   Writing is subjective; so is editing. Sometimes the reasons for rejection are so subtle that they are difficult to explain. Other times, they are so complex (involving such things as list development, demographics, budgeting, line focus, shifts in the industry, etc.) that they are...well...difficult to explain. It takes much less time just to say no.

2. **Cowardice**. Because we hate to argue. Editors are notoriously conflict adverse. We like our conflict in manuscripts, not in email or on the phone. And the minute we start sending explanations, someone will want to argue with us.

Sending a note that says, "Your characters need more depth and a broader view on life" often results in an angry email with selected passages intended to prove the judgment wrong. Or a phone message venting about our abilities to judge any kind of literary work. I've lost track of how many times I've been asked for a second chance, even though I've left no opening to do so. Like most editors I know, if I think a rewrite would make acceptance possible, I will make it clear that I'm open to that.

Not all writers are professionals who know they need to vent to critique groups. And editors don't like being beat up, even unreasonably, for our skills. No more than writers do.

3. **Perspective**. An editor is one person. One opinion. One judge. And we don't always agree with each other. Plus, our publishing houses have differing goals. House "tones" vary from one another. A book that's wrong for Baker might be fine with Thomas Nelson/Harper Collins. So I could easily suggest a change for a book that an editor at Bethany would ask be reverted. And don't even get me started on editorial arguments about prologues. During a mentoring session, I once told an author I thought her prologue was a needless distraction. She immediately started sobbing—which startled me. I hadn't been *that* mean about it. Then she explained she had added the prologue at the request of a well-known editor at a large house.

As I said: one editor equals one opinion. This means that personal comments, in the long run, could be a waste of everyone's time, yours as well as ours.

If you want to know if your work is lousy, join a critique group, submit to a contest, or take a course. That's what they're for. If you really want to know why your book doesn't fit a particular house, study that publisher's fiction titles for the past three years, talk to authors who've sold to them, and review bestseller lists. If you have a dream publisher, you should be doing this anyway.

In the meantime, keep submitting.

Those form rejections will continue, frustrating though they may be. They are the easiest way to keep your manuscript in circulation until it does find the right home.

WHAT PART OF "NO" DON'T YOU UNDERSTAND?

"No" is a complete sentence.

Anne Lamott

For most writers, "No" involves rejection. Agents say no. Publishers say no. As a result, it becomes one of the most difficult words in our vocabulary. We don't like it when folks say no to us; we understand the disappointment that comes with it, and we dislike passing on that feeling.

The truth is, however, that "No" will become one of the most important weapons in our careers. It will help us identify and set boundaries that will support us and help us grow as writers—and as business people.

Boundaries to Set

"A simple favor," she said. Since I wrote short stories, could she "borrow one" to follow as an example? Of course! My ego flattered, I lent her a post-apocalyptic tale I'd worked on for months. When I found out she'd turned it in for an English assignment—and

gotten an A—I felt a heart-breaking betrayal that she did not understand. Even after I explained why this had basically ended our friendship, the only thing on her face was confusion.

Lesson learned. Not only did I need to set boundaries around my words but also around my *ability* to write. Perfecting those boundaries didn't come easy. It still doesn't. But my voice is my own, and I've worked hard for many years to develop it. It is mine to give in whatever way I see fit, but it remains *my* gift from God, and I need to use it responsibly. For me to use it irresponsibly— or for someone else to claim it as their own—is to disrespect a precious gift from the Lord.

Not to mention that the last part is illegal. Plagiarism *can* land you in front of a judge.

Likewise, using your gift responsibly means *producing*. You need to set goals and cordon off time to write. You need to approach your writing in the same way you would with any job, fencing off time to do it without letting the busyness of life take it away.

Setting boundaries around the ability to sculpt other people's words—a gift for editing—can be even harder. "Can you take a quick look at this?" has become a dreaded question in my world. While I don't mind helping most folks who ask this outside the purview of my job, it's a rocky shore.

People who are not writers by trade often don't understand the nature of editing; they just want you to check for typos. But what if their typo-laden cover letter is also a mangled mess of prose that will leave a bad impression on a prospective boss? Where's the line between hurting feelings and genuinely helping?

Boundaries to Keep

Your gift for words is precious beyond measure. Whether you've perfected your craft or you're still discovering the beauty in your words, *never* forget that. Writing well is never easy; it takes long hours of practice, study, and emotional torment, but every minute is worth it. Getting to the point when words soar into your soul produces a euphoria unlike any other.

Do not let anyone belittle this or take advantage of it. If anyone in your life says, "Well, anyone can write," walk away from them. (I usually have to or run the risk of doing them bodily harm.)

And don't let anyone cajole you by saying, "You're good with words. You need to write this for me." Or even "I have an idea for a book you can write." **Just say no**. In addition to being dishonest, they are *stealing* your time and your creativity. (My response to this is usually to remind them that this is my profession, and I get a flat $75 fee for anything up to 300 words. Rates after that are negotiable.)

Protect your goals and your time to write. Believe me, I know how life, family, and a dozen other responsibilities can steal time and delay goals. I've failed by dropping this boundary more than any other. It's easy to do. But you need to honor your gift by actually sitting down at the keyboard and using it.

Boundaries to Break

But life is not always kind and gentle to writers—or their families. Sometimes there is blood. Or a broken heart. In addition to our gift for words, God has also granted most of us a sense of wisdom. The friend who's been out of work for several months needs

your help more than she needs a lecture on the nature of your profession. The teenager who's been dumped needs kind guidance and broad shoulders right this very minute. A fellow writer needs brainstorming help that he may one day return in kind.

While we need to set boundaries, we do not exist behind high walls.

Whether you're laying out boundaries—or carefully stepping over them—call on God for good judgment. And, above all, never *ever* feel bad about just saying *no*.

PROFESSIONALISM

The difference between ordinary and extraordinary is that little extra.

Jimmy Johnson

Writing is both art and craft, a combination of talent, perseverance, and hard-won skills. It is mostly done alone. Publishing, on the other hand, is a community effort, one that depends on each individual to do their job with precision and professionalism. Writing is personal and grounded in the heart, but it must work within a business environment in order to reach the most readers. This means writers must approach their work with the same professionalism as the editors and marketers who help them reach the broadest possible range of readers. Creativity is precious and needs to be protected—but not at the cost of reputation and skills.

I am a writer. I am also an editor, but I was a writer before I became an editor. I love both crafts with a passion that runs deep. I care. I care that the work is the best it can be. The *words* come first, and I care that writers are nurtured and allowed to grow in

the ways that are best for them and their calling. I care that the nurturing comes not only from fellow writers but from agents and editors who can help further writing careers.

Which is why I hate when relationships break down due to a lack of professionalism. Or worse, a lack of patience.

Before I go on, you should know I have had moments of unprofessionalism myself. I know how it feels. When I misbehave, I am so ashamed that I usually compound the situation by hiding and going silent. This is a mistake, and I'm still paying for the last couple of incidents. I have a professional relationship, an extremely beneficial one, that remains at risk because of my own behavior.

So I know it happens despite the best intentions.

But I've been in this business long enough to know that it also happens *intentionally*. I've seen writers almost destroy careers with their behavior. I've known folks who, despite repeated warnings from agents or fellow writers, have let their ego, or their impatience, or their dreams, kill relationships with publishers who only want the best for them.

I know authors I hope I never have to work with.

The reasons for that statement are varied, and this chapter comes about from not only my thirty-plus years in the business but some extensive conversations with other editors and agents about author behavior.

Yeah, if you haven't figured this out yet, you should realize that editors and agents talk to each other. A lot.

Here are a few issues that come up:

Refusal to respond to editorial suggestions. Editors and agents don't make changes or suggested changes for personal reasons. We know we're working on your baby. But our minds are on the readers and the book buyers, and our opinions are based on years of work with other manuscripts. Editorial suggestions are not made because we dislike your work; instead, our goal is to make it the best it can be. When an author ignores a change, especially a major one, without feedback, the editor begins to think the author has no interest in improving. This bespeaks an ego and stubbornness that can show up in other areas of the relationship. It's a major red flag. If you don't like the editing, start a conversation. Don't just turn in a revision that ignores or stets them with no explanation.

Impatience. The publishing process is slow. As a writer you must understand this. This drives some authors to self-publish, and some self-publishing authors do find success in this route. But moving too quickly—publishing without going through an editorial and proofreading process, for instance—can stall or delay a career. Word of mouth about a badly written or edited book published too soon can kill sales of future works. Whatever path you choose, take the time to make your book the best it can be.

High maintenance. Folks ask what I mean by this all the time, and the answer is usually, "The same thing that makes someone high maintenance in the rest of life." It starts with the attitude that "I'm special, so I should have all your attention" and continues with "It's *my* book; I know what's best for it."

As an in-house editor, I am responsible for as many as forty new books a year, plus the ones just published and the ones two to three

years out. I receive more than three hundred submissions a year from agents and authors. I'm making plans for conferences and handling all the administrative duties that go with my job. No one author is going to have all my attention. An agent with a list of forty or more clients will be handling the same balancing act.

And if you know what's best for your book, then I'd suggest you do seriously consider self-publishing. Otherwise, trust that a publisher is in the business of getting as many books as possible into the hands of readers. They have a lot of experience in how that happens, and sometimes their experience will stand in opposition to what you want. Learn to trust.

Refusal to take career advice. This one is a bit of a corollary to "high maintenance," but it goes a step further, and I hear it more from agents than other editors. While launching a career is slow, for instance, your work will pick up increasing speed as time goes on. You'll go from waiting several years for the first couple of books to having an editor want a book every three to six months. Life will become a minefield of deadlines, edits, marketing, traveling, and speaking. Skilled agents can guide you through this with wisdom...if you let them.

One of the best analogies I've heard recently (and apologies to the originator of this; I don't remember!) is that the beginning of a writer's publishing career is like college and graduate school. It involves years of work, learning, networking, writing, and waiting. Then more writing and waiting. Once the career is launched, however, life can change in a hurry.

And, just as it would be with an MBA grad, a writer will be working with a series of professional colleagues. You may be in a home

office in your pajamas, cat on your lap, writing on the book of your heart—but we will expect you to act with the same professionalism as our colleagues down the hall.

If you don't, the difficult work of getting published on a regular basis will get a whole lot harder.

NEW YEAR'S *REVOLUTIONS*

There is no education like adversity.

Disraeli

N
o, that's not a typo. Let's talk *revolutions*, instead, the kind that turn our world upside down.

I don't make New Year's resolutions. Haven't for years, since I realized I was layering on my own guilt trip when I couldn't keep them. While some folks are great habit-keepers or habit-breakers, I'm not. I don't even get up at the same time every morning. The closest I've come to a habit is placing my toothbrush in the same place. Usually.

So making a declaration that I'm going to develop or break a habit (lose weight, exercise regularly, etc.) is built-in failure. Why do that to myself?

Not to mention that the first part of the year seems particularly inclined to *revolutions*—"life events" that turn all our plans inside out—I see this in a lot of people. Winter brings on illnesses. Christmas bills pile up. People fall on the ice. Schools close for

snow days. Budget cuts mean job losses. Cold weather brings broken pipes and other unexpected home repairs. Shorter days bring on depressions.

Basically, after Christmas, we're all exhausted! Renewal, the idea of pushing beyond the problems and doldrums, turns into a pipe dream, and we fight just to regain normality. Often our character is revealed by how we handle the upheavals. I'm about average in that regard...in some things I do well. Others...not so much.

One thing that often gets set aside is my writing. While the drive to write lives in me like a hungry animal, the creative juices get zapped by the trials. This result is that I get a little more nuts than usual.

And I'm definitely not alone. Life happens to all of us.

"So You Say You Want a Revolution"

It's easy to let the "revolutions" in our lives derail us from our goals. Whether they are unpleasant—like a hospital stay—or whether they are joyous—like the birth of a child or grandchild. Whether it's a disruption or a permanent change to a "new normal," staying on our chosen path can be more difficult than we ever imagined.

I've had more than enough experience with this, so I've learned to...

- **Set priorities and be brutal about it.** People around you aren't going to like all your choices. Stick to it and follow your heart. If friends abandon you because of it, good riddance. Grieve them and move on.

- **Understand the difference between temporary and permanent derailments**. Temporary ones are setbacks; the permanents mean choosing a new way of life. Pray for wisdom and acceptance.

- **Set goals.** If you can't write right now, set a date for a restart. It may be ambitious, but be determined.

- **Don't be afraid to dream—and to dream BIG**. I want to finish three books this year. I'm off to a rocky start. But that's OK. Once a month, I'll adjust my schedule and see where I am. Day-to-day accountability is a great way to track progress, but it also keeps the endgame in mind.

- **Pray for wisdom and guidance.** Sometimes, when the car hits the ditch, we just pray for strength and endurance. But wisdom and guidance for the right choices is vital during this time. God has big shoulders. It's OK to cry a little. Or a lot.

- *Know* **you will persevere.** You are a child of God. He will get you through this. Together you can accomplish more than you can possibly imagine.

My book of devotions, *My Mother's Quilt*, came out three weeks after my daughter died. To say I was worthless in terms of marketing is an understatement. I was numb—completely frozen—for more than three months. But I had to trust God and do what I could. To date, it's been my most successful nonfiction book, and I refuse to ponder the "what ifs" of that time. I'd had a revolution in my life, and God walked me through it.

He can walk you through it as well, no matter what.

CHANGE OF PLANS

Expect the best, plan for the worst, and prepare to be surprised.

Denis Waitley

It's one of those social media posters that makes the rounds. On one side is a little stick figure on a bike, headed up a long steep mountain. It's labeled: "Your plans for success." On the other side is a stick figure on a bike weathering storms, valleys, turns, gaps, etc. It's labeled: "Reality."

This is misleading. Oh, it's got a good goal in mind: to remind folks that the path to real success is never smooth. What's misleading about it is that on both sides...the top of the mountain is the same. The road may be rough, but the goal never waivers.

For some people, this may, in fact, be "reality." And some folks actually do live the first side...a straight shot.

But for many of us not only is the road rough, the destination shifts as well. You may start up Mount Everest only to discover you've arrived at the top of Mount Kilimanjaro, wandering in a confused daze and wondering how you got there.

Even though it is exactly where you needed to be, after all is said and done.

I, for instance, knew from an early age I wanted to be a writer. At first, I wanted to write mysteries (Nancy Drew and Robin Kane ruled!). Then biographies (I was in love with Daniel Boone). Then romance (hormones, what can we say?). Then science fiction (Robert Heinlein and Harlan Ellison changed my life). Then...

- "You should be a teacher. You're very good at this." (This is true. I love to teach. I just hate grading papers and creating lesson plans.)
- "You need a career. You don't want to work at Orange Julius while you wait to get published." (This was a college recruiter. Few comments have ever made me so mad or so determined.)
- "A writer? Really? You know you need a fallback plan." (My mother worried. It was her job.)

Sigh. As for most of the rest of the planet, my problem was two-fold. I needed money for regular stuff (food, rent), but I had already witnessed too many writers who gave up their dreams because a day-to-day job ate their creative fervor. And their time.

So I turned to publishing, with the goal of learning the business with a "non-creative" job, while I wrote at night. I did, working my way up from editorial secretary to editor...which is a lot like being a teacher without quite so many hassles. And while I've made money writing (I've published...oh, let's see...mysteries, romances, devotionals, biographical sketches, and the occasional piece of science fiction), I don't make my living at it. Yet. But I've

never stopped, and sometimes my view from the top of Mount Kilimanjaro looks like the best of all worlds.

So...Where Are You On That Path?

In my writing classes, I often press, to rephrase *Finding Nemo*'s Dory, "Just keep writing, just keep writing." But I often talk to authors who are completely discouraged because they haven't met their writing goals.

- The process takes too long.
- They're into their third book, or fifth, with no sale.
- They can't get an agent.
- Why keep on?

Why? Two main reasons. One, your plans are not God's plans. His success is not your success. Two, you're either a writer or you're not. If you're a writer, then you're going to write, even if no one *ever* sees it. And that's OK. That part is between you and God.

But there's a third reason I encourage writers not to give up, which is a corollary to the first one. You may be headed in the wrong direction with *the readers* you need to reach. You may have a story for the ages, but God intends it mostly for your own family or someone close to you He needs to reach. If you're writing about a crisis or a God-inspired survival, your story may not yet be finished.

My idea of success was to be the next Sue Grafton or Octavia Butler. Nothing less would satisfy...I thought. But while I may never have a bestseller or be a household name, I feel quite successful with my journey because I've allowed God to direct not only what

I do but also my definition of success. So far. But I still have more to do.

So do you.

So when I say, "Just keep writing," it's a multilayered message. Take a deep look at where God is leading you as well as your own desires.

And I'll be waiting for you on the top of Mount Kilimanjaro.

A LIFE OF WRITING

To survive, you must tell stories.

Umberto Eco

One of my favorite authors turned 82 at the end of May 2015. He had suffered a lot of illnesses in the few months prior to that, including a stroke. Yet he was still writing and selling his work, marketing it on social media and YouTube. Another favorite will turn 82 in 2020, and she still writes three books a year, doing so by sitting at her desk six days a week. Her last novels hit the *New York Times* bestseller list.

I've not reached their age or stature in the literary world, but I well know that when (if!) I do, I'll still be typing/scribbling/dreaming of new plots and characters. I've already been doing this most of my life and getting paid in some form or fashion for editing or writing for almost forty years. I've been blessed by being in the right places at the right times, but I've also had a drive to write that I now recognize as a call from God.

It's a passion, one that runs so deep that I've already investigated devices that can help me should my eyesight dim or I become

unable to type. This passion drives the choices I make in other areas of my life, from where I live to which movies I see or concerts I attend. I don't have a lot of retirement funds set aside, so as I contemplate the later years in my life, I have faith that the call God entrusted to me will still allow me to earn enough to support myself.

And stay busy. I've long known that one secret to a longer, healthier life is to stay busy. Not to "finish" a career, then sit down, turn on the television, and veg out. My mother quilted, did puzzles, and read hefty novels until she was 87. Grandma Moses didn't start painting until she was 77 and famously said, "Painting's not important. The important thing is keeping busy." With the number of plots and characters jumbling through my head every day, I can't imagine running out of anything to write about.

Most of the writers I know are the same way. We *need* to write. To be honest, it doesn't matter if we began writing at 7 or 77. When that passion strikes, it invests us with a drive to share our words, our hearts, our stories. Even our friends and family start recognizing this. Writing may be a solitary effort, but our world gets quickly drawn into what we do. I get so out of sorts when I don't write, my non-writing friends start whispering, "Have you written anything lately?"

Never mistake: ***this is a gift***. Yes, it is also a talent and a skill, one we work hard at. But the ability to use words to touch minds and hearts is precious and rare. Embrace it and the life it leads to, no matter how long you've been on the planet.

Left Fin, Right Turn, Keep Swimming

A word after a word after a word is power.

Margaret Atwood

The deep gloom of the theater meant no one could see my tears, but I knew my friend could hear me gasping for air. She'd already glanced at me awkwardly, unsure of whether to say anything. So I turned to her and whispered, "I can't believe I'm sobbing over an animated *fish!*"

The movie was *Finding Nemo*, and Nemo's mom, Coral, had just met her fate defending her young. And, of course, I wasn't really crying over a deceased clown fish but over all the moms who had ever sacrificed for their children. Who had stood in the face of danger and given up so much. Their stories were as embedded in me as though they were my own, gifts of the storytellers who had come before and left so much behind. This is what we do as writers. We leave behind the influential messages of our culture.

I also resonated a lot with Dori, the blue tang with the short-term memory problem. She resembles a lot in my life as I seek to compose and share those cultural tales. First, I'm easily distracted. Just ask anyone who's tried to have a single focused conversation with me. But second, and most importantly, I learned a long time ago that if I am going to have any kind of success in this business, I have to "just keep swimming."

Quite frequently, such as when my bio is read at conferences, I'm asked, "How have you done so much?" The answer is simple: I'm old, and I never turn down an opportunity to learn something new—or a writing or editorial job I've never tackled before. Part of this philosophy is borne out of unlimited curiosity; the rest comes from pure desperation—aka, I was broke.

Training Ground

I have always wanted to be a writer and editor, even as a kid. My dream jobs. My first job after college, however, was in the sales and catering department of a Hyatt Regency, and I gave serious thought to making hospitality my career path. But an editorial secretary position opened at Abingdon Press, and I applied, hoping to make the leap to my "true love." I learned more about writing and publishing in the next four years than I could have in any other job. When that job ended, I found myself heading up *Ideals* magazine at the tender age of twenty-eight. Then, after a short stint as a stay-at-home mom, I went back to an editor's job, which lasted less than two years.

In the meantime, I wrote more than 300 short stories, most not worth publishing. But a few did see print, along with some biographical sketches, devotionals, Bible studies, etc. My freelance

career was in its infancy, but I continued to accept jobs and build my network. When I accepted a position at Thomas Nelson in 1992, I kept the freelance side going, although it was sidelined after my divorce for a few years. One of those "life happens" phases in life. But when I picked it up again, it grew—slowly since it wasn't my main focus. But grow it did.

I sold my first book of devotionals in 1999, and beginning in 2000, I was once again a stay-at-home mom, single this time. For the next five years, I edited anything that wasn't illegal or immoral, and sold my first two novels. I dedicate myself to submitting five queries a day for six weeks, with unbelievable results. I stopped submitting queries only when I had to write to deadlines!

Not everything I attempted went rosily along, however. Freelance work has an ebb and flow to it that not everyone can manage, and I often didn't balance my responsibilities to my daughter with my publishing job as well as I should have. I declared bankruptcy at one point, and then things got really bad. Staring at a check book with only $1.87 in it sent me to my knees in prayer. God came through yet again with a phone call. I realized the time had come for more corporate work, and I rejoined Thomas Nelson in 2005.

Yes, the temptation had been there to just give up and do something else. When you're flat broke and the only way is up, any job looks good. Why not go back to the hotel industry and start over?

Because I Am a Writer

Any thoughts of changing careers lasted less than a day. I don't know if I'd be good at anything else because my heart would not be in it—and I am distinctly spoiled in a first world kind of way.

Even when the adverb "barely" always slipped in front of "making it," I know that this was the river in which I had to "keep swimming," even when a damaged left fin (a bad choice) made me make constant right turns. And that perseverance paid off, leading me to the two jobs I'd craved for my entire life: fiction editor and author. I'm now in a position where I go to conferences and speak to writers, network with publishers and agents, and spend my life with great books. I have a new book coming out soon. I'm working on two more.

Seriously. There is nothing better.

Yes. It took a long time to get here. More than thirty years.

Most people don't want to wait that long, and that's up to them. Not all paths are the same. Some get to where they want to be quicker; some take longer than I did. SPEED isn't the point.

The journey is the point, and following the path you believe God has in store for your life. Listening to His voice and guidance. Spreading the messages that impact our world.

The point...is to keep swimming. Upstream. And never give up.

Part Two

The End Is Never the End:
A Finished Manuscript Is Only
the Beginning

God's Timing Is Perfect

Yet God has made everything beautiful for its own time. He has planted eternity in the human heart, but even so, people cannot see the whole scope of God's work from beginning to end.

Ecclesiastes 3:11

From 2000–2005, I worked as a freelance editor. I worked for a number of different publishers, editing just about any subject matter you can imagine. I edited for big-name folks and for companies no longer in business. During this time, I edited a publisher-contracted book called *Angel Falls* by Connie Mann. A debut novel, but extremely well written. This book pushed the edges a bit for Christian fiction, with both character arcs and setting, but I loved every word. I worked closely with the author, and we smoothed out the rough spots and toned down some of the "edginess." I turned it into the editor and put the check in the bank.

Then came the oddest phone call. The editor remained concerned about the subject matter. I reviewed the manuscript again.

Connie and I worked on it a second time. Still, the concerns lingered. Finally, Connie and I both took the position that if we removed the elements that created the most concern, it would rip out the heart of the book. The publisher agreed.

They killed the book.

I was angry and frustrated. Connie was devastated. She'd written for six years, working hard to learn her craft, and this was the book of her heart. Which, apparently, no one wanted.

I went on to edit other things, but not for that publisher. Connie stopped writing. In her words:

> To say I was crushed would be putting it mildly. I'd been writing for about six years then and had stacks of rejections before getting the "yes" on this one. Having it rejected when I'd come so close was devastating. Due to serious family and financial issues, coupled with this rejection, I became a boat captain and didn't write for several years. I couldn't.

Connie, however, is a writer. A good one. And when God puts words on your heart, you don't ignore them for long.

> But as with most of us, the stories pulled me back. I started writing again and sold *Trapped!* to The Wild Rose Press and then worked on the movie, *Catch of a Lifetime.* But *Angel Falls* has always been the "book of my heart."

Time goes by. I didn't forget, however, and neither did Connie. I worked at Thomas Nelson for four years, then freelanced

another eighteen months. When I became the fiction editor at Abingdon Press in August 2010, I emailed Connie to see if *Angel Falls* had sold.

The day I sent the email, a copy of the manuscript landed on my desk. Like minds, I guess. Or God in the machine.

I read it—it was as good as I'd remembered. I couldn't propose it yet; our list was full, and a lot of changes were going on. The months went by. I was promoted to senior acquisitions editor. The in-house shifts and changes began to settle. Then, one day, a spot opened up on an already full list.

> I sent it to [Ramona], and another one-and-a-half years passed while she championed it with the publishing house. Then I got an email from her that began, "I know you thought this day would never come..."

Looking back, I think the concerns of the previous publisher were spot on. At the time, foreign settings were not in demand, and the issue of healing from past sexual abuse was almost unheard of in CBA fiction, especially in the context of a fast-paced romantic suspense novel. Regina, the heroine in *Angel Falls*, is one of the most unique main characters I've ever read in Christian fiction. She's not just feisty; she's *fierce.*

Regina grew up in the slums of Brazil and was head of an orphanage. Her faith in God as Savior is unshakable, and her life is all about the children. She carries a knife at all times and will do anything she can to save children from the fate she suffered as a child. She's paired with Brooks Anderson, an American soldier who's almost as damaged as she is. Their bond is a toddler

someone wants dead. Badly. What results is a wild ride through the jungle in order to save the child—and each other. The fact that they begin to heal each other on the way winds up being essential to their ultimate goal.

Despite the fact that it's a high-quality, tautly written story (I lost a couple of fingernails on the first read-through), it might not have been well received all those years ago. But trends change, as do the expectations of readers.

Angel Falls released in Spring 2013—almost a *decade* from the time I first saw it and much, much longer than that since Connie began writing it with a dream in her heart.

So, for every writer who is still waiting, I think Connie says it best:

> If you are discouraged today, I hope this will encourage you. Never, ever, ever, *ever* give up on the dreams God has planted in your heart. His timing may not be ours, but it's always perfect.

DOES IT TAKE A MIRACLE TO SELL A MANUSCRIPT AT A CONFERENCE?

I'd like to have money. And I'd like to be a good writer. These two can come together, and I hope they will, but if that's too adorable, I'd rather have money.

Dorothy Parker

If you've pitched and pitched and been to a dozen conferences, still with no results, you may wonder if the answer to this question is yes, even though you've heard stories of novels bought in the food line.

But the truth behind those stories is that the novel wasn't really *sold* in the food line. That's just where the connection was made, author to editor or author to agent. The editor or agent hears a good pitch and asks to see something more. The encounter in the food line leads to a lot of emails, a lot of reading, some committee meetings, a business plan or two, *then* the book is bought via contract.

And it *does* happen. While at Abingdon Press I signed more than one author I first met at the Blue Ridge Mountains Christian Writers Conference. One author wound up writing four books for me, and, yes, all four of these sales are a direct result from meeting her at BRMCWC, getting to know her heart and her work, and realizing her potential. She has an agent now, but I would have signed her with or without one.

And then there's Yvonne.

Now, if you've ever been to BRMCWC, you know Yvonne Lehman. (If you've been around Christian publishing for a while, you might know her because she's one of the most prolific writers I've ever known.) She's the founding director of the conference and an unforgettable personality. Yvonne and I have known each other for a while, and I greatly admire her work. But when she sat beside me at one of the worship services, it was literally a matter of God putting us together at the right time.

You see, just before the 2011 conference, the fiction team I headed at Abingdon brainstormed trends and ideas for books. Our sales director asked about the possibility of having a book for the upcoming anniversary of a well-known historic tragedy. I didn't exactly laugh, but I do remember my reply being a bit snarky about the time frame involved. Given our catalog and promotional schedule, what he suggested would take a miracle. And I said so.

Ahem. Yes, don't remind me.

Enter Yvonne, who plopped down next to me at the conference a few weeks later. We chatted, then out of the blue, she said, "You wouldn't by any chance want a book about the Titanic, would you?"

I stared at her. "What have you got?" She told me, and I said, send it to me. "I'll read it tonight."

She did, and I did. I forwarded it to our sales director and associate publisher with a timeline that would make it happen. The next afternoon, I had their yes. By the time I got home, we had a business plan. Yvonne went to writing, and I worked out the details with her agent. Yvonne wrote something like 130,000 words from May to the end of June, then cut it to our word count, and we put it on a crash course through production.

Hearts That Survive released in March 2012.

A miracle? Well, not really. More like God's timing and some seriously hard work from a talented author. But it was definitely a sale that would not have happened if it weren't for the God-driven connection two people made at a writer's conference.

And that's real key to those "miracles." Hard work, a cuppa talent, a lot of preparation, and networking with the people God puts together.

Speed Dating—Editorial Style

Is it possible to be ticket for going too fast during speed dating?

Neil Leckman

So...is it really possible for a ten-minute mentoring appointment to do any good?"

Hm. This question came to me many times after I had stopped taking pitches as an acquisitions editor and began working as a freelance editor in 2015. A few conferences asked me to take mentoring appointments, including the Florida Christian Writers Conference. So the benefits of mentoring have been large on my mind.

My answer, however, may sound a bit like a cop-out: Yes, it can make a difference, but it depends a lot on the writer.

Choosing Wisely

Mentors are usually selected by a conference committee for their experience, knowledge, and proven ability to help other writers.

They are all qualified to help on some level. But they are not all equal. If you write, for instance, young adult speculative fiction, it's not going to be wise for you to choose someone who specializes in devotionals or nonfiction.

Before signing up for an appointment at a conference—or hiring a mentor privately—check out the mentor's website (if they have one), bio on the conference website...or just ask. Most mentors are willing to tell you if they can help or suggest you have a sit-down with Susan May Warren or Michelle Medlock Adams instead.

Ask Wisely

Carefully plan out what you wish to discuss beforehand. Be as specific as possible. Tell the mentor right away what genre you write and what your concerns are. Skip such questions as "What do you think the trends in romance will be over the next five years?" and dig deep in a way that will benefit you and your book.

- "I write romantic suspense. Do you think a hidden baby story is too clichéd?"
- "I really need the reader to know this info. How do I avoid a backstory dump?"
- "Is it really impossible to be successful in two or three genres? Do I have to focus?"
- "I've written myself into a corner. Can you look at this scene and give me some tips?"

Be Willing to LISTEN

More than a few writers have sat down in front of me and want little more than for me to tell them what they're doing right. Which I *will* do. They don't, however, want to hear the hard truths: what they need to do in order to improve, to push themselves as writers, and to aim toward publication.

Despite what many people think, writing is not a natural skill. Storytelling can be (although it can also be learned), but writing those stories with in-depth craft skills is most certainly a learned prospect. And with anything we learn, we can continue to learn more.

But we have to be willing to hear what's being said, good or bad.

Be Willing to WORK

Taking the tips and suggestions from a mentor is more than scribbling them down during an interview. It's absorbing them. Testing them. Seeing if they truly apply to what you're doing as a writer, and—if they are—putting them into action. It means looking more critically at your own skills and stories and doing the work to push them to a higher level.

So, yes, having a mentoring appointment at a conference can be exceptionally beneficial. But like any step on your writing journey, you have to remain open to the experience and fold the information into the larger mix that is your mind for storytelling. Butter and sugar are yummy, but they only become cake when you finish the recipe.

THE 40-PERCENT SOLUTION

Doing business without advertising is like winking at a girl in the dark. You know what you are doing, but nobody else does.

Steuart Henderson Britt

Cristine Bolley and Cheryl Sloan Wray changed my career forever with two simple bits of advice. And lest you think the workshops at smaller conferences aren't as insightful, I heard both the same weekend at the Southern Christian Writers Conference, which is held every June in Tuscaloosa, Alabama. Although the conference has grown every year, there were about sixty in attendance when I heard this. Small conference; major lessons.

In this case, their advice stunned me—and kicked my butt into gear.

From Cristine: Successful writers will spend about 40 percent of their work time marketing. Before publication, you need to spend it trying to sell yourself and your work to editors and

agents, starting a platform. After publication, you'll spend it selling your books to readers, expanding that platform.

From Cheryl: If you want to be successful, you need to set a goal of submitting at least **five** queries a day. Yes, five per **day**.

Now...I wouldn't be surprised if you are currently having the same reaction I did. My expression at the time was the one my mother always responded to with, "Shut your mouth, dear. You're letting flies in."

You see, I was suffering under the impression that a writer succeeded by writing.

Silly me.

Sounds impossible, doesn't it? How in the world do you get any actual **writing** done if you're doing all that marketing?

By remembering that if you don't do it, you're just winking in the dark. Cute, but who'll see it?

You can start by taking a look at your schedule to see when you're most creative...and when you're not. I'm a night owl by nature, which means my best writing occurs between 4 p.m. and midnight. Mornings are lousy for me. I don't think clearly. Please don't ask me to create or decide—even on breakfast.

So mornings are a good time for me to focus on the career aspects of my writing; that's when I'd do my marketing and brainstorming. After hearing their advice, I set new goals for that time. I'd research my dream publishers (magazine or book) and agents (book). Then I'd gather all the info I could about them. What they were buying, who they were buying, who's the editor I needed to touch base with.

I'd do a little bit of that information gathering every day, growing the lists constantly. Then I'd spend time brainstorming book and magazine ideas and running those under the list of potential publishers. Draft query letters.

By that time, I would be ready to write. So I'd go write.

Once I completed that first manuscript and wrote the synopsis, I refined the query letters and sent off the first five. Then added to the list. Every morning, I focused on selling. Every afternoon, I worked on the next manuscript.

I finished the second before getting a nibble on the first, which just increased my morning efforts. I refined the query letters for the first one and worked on the ones for the second. Now I had **two** finished manuscripts to brag about.

Yes, I got lots of rejections, but requests for full proposals or manuscripts started arriving as well. I started sending them off as soon as I could get them out the door. Sending out seventy-five queries took less than a month, and I received three requests for more material.

And I sold. Three months after I went on Cristine and Cheryl's combined plan, I had sold three articles and had two book contracts in hand.

The Next Step

OK, so now what? The final edit is finished and off to its intended recepient. Time to relax and wait for the book and all the ensuing praises, right?

You're joking, *right?*

Most of us already know that the times when a publisher put a lot of time and dollars behind marketing new books have slipped away like ice on glass. These days an author will control much of the publicity about her book and drive most of the marketing.

But, you protest, I don't have a lot of money for mailings and websites. I barely pay the rent!

Don't worry. As a newly published author, you don't really have to spend a lot of money. The big key in building a reader database and higher visibility for your book isn't money.

It's **time**.

Forty percent of your time, in fact—that part of your time you used to spend trying to sell your manuscript to publishers will now be spent selling your book to readers. You need to put as much—if not more—effort into selling to *readers* as you did to *editors.*

And if you choose to self-publish, this is even more vital.

There are so many free tools you can use to promote your book, it's mindboggling, and it doesn't stop with social media and giveaways. The online world is also filled with articles on how to build a social network, set up free blogs, get involved with a blog tour or blogger interviews. There are a number of other sites that can help you, along with other resources. Edie Melson has a wealth of books and blog posts about online marketing, and she and DiAnn Mills even run a conference centered on it. Do a little research, and you'll find tips galore. Seriously consider joining support groups, online readers groups, or writers groups such as Word Weavers, American Christian Fiction Writers, Mystery Writers

of America, or Sisters in Crime. All these organizations have scores of resources to help authors promote their genres.

Most publishers have a team member who can get you started by filling out forms and working with them on their efforts. If you haven't heard from them as the publication date closes in, contact your editor and/or the marketing team at the publisher and tell them you're available for any of their efforts. Ask if there's a form they need you to fill out about future events. Ask if there are specific things they want you to do. Focus first there.

Then set about researching all the free stuff and making a plan. A *reasonable* plan for you, your time, and your family.

Then set it all aside and spend some time in prayer.

Pray? About *marketing*? About convincing people to spend money?

Yes. Because this isn't about them spending money.

It's about *you* using ***your gift from God***. You have been given something precious. God's message in your heart. It comes out in your words, your stories. Your words are salt and light and you do *not* put them under a basket (Luke 11).

Marketing is showing people what you have. Asking them to read your book is asking them to engage in a much larger conversation. You don't sit around winking in the dark and telling yourself how well you write. You're out there to show them what God has done for you—and what He can do for them.

You get out there...and make it *shine*.

He'll take it from there.

BITING THE MARKETING BULLET

Your brand is so much more than what you sell.

Jon Iwata

This is the part that never gets any easier, no matter how long you do it. And, yes, I have been doing this for a *long* time. I have survived the days of paper manuscripts and SASEs. Of waiting for more than a year for a rejection. Of form letters, postcards, and postage. I've had stories rejected with a one-inch sticky note that had "Not for us" as one of the multiple options to be checked.

Rejections haven't changed much, but acceptances and publishing have. I remember the days of magazine ads, huge sales conferences, author appearances, and big marketing budgets. When publishers handled most of the marketing and all authors had to do was write...what?

Oh, yeah...*those* days never really existed. I remember that too. The myth of the author in the writing closet who never had to

market a book was born from the romantic image of J. D. Salinger and other reclusives whose popularity was the result of a bolt of lightning and endless numbers of English teachers.

The rest of us have to work for it. Seriously.

Have you noticed how much marketing James Patterson does? Or Neil Gaiman? You think they're out there interacting with folks because they're extroverts who can't wait to get out from behind the typewriter? Have you noticed that they mention titles less often than the type of fiction they write?

So I have a book coming out soon...and marketing it scares me to death. Every time I load Facebook or Instagram, I feel completely overwhelmed and intimidated. I really would prefer the cabin in the woods, emerging every six months to get supplies and pick up mail. Unfortunately, that's not our world anymore.

So how do I "gird my loins" for the marketing battle?

Deep breaths help. Prayer. I put on the "Ramona the marketer" hat the same way I put on a character before stepping on stage. And I *try* to make reasonable choices, given my limited budget, time, and energy level. That last one is truly key in keeping this under control. Some people have lots of it. But I can take "laconic" to a whole new level.

- I set reasonable expectations by evaluating exactly how much I can do, given my other responsibilities.
- I limit my social media. For this next book I'm focusing on Facebook and Twitter, with Instagram when I can remember it. This is why...

- I've hired a marketing firm to help. They specialize in blog tours and social media, and they don't cost an arm and a leg. It's well within my budget. Speaking of...

- I budgeted a reasonable amount for marketing and started saving a little out of each paycheck over the past few months. I won't overspend. When it's done, I'm done. For this book, that's $500, and I'm closing in on the end of that. What's left is reserved for mailing books to my launch team and endorsers.

- I asked friends for help. I created a reader page, and I let folks know upfront what I'll do for them and what I'll expect in return. They can opt in...or not. I well know that people have time limitations.

- I focus as much on my brand as the book. I write suspense. I want people to connect that word with my work.

And that's pretty much it. This is what I can do for now. I'll take notes, learn from the goofs, and try to do more for the next suspense book.

Do what you can. Then stop. Part of being a productive writer is taking care of yourself, your time, and your energy. The rest is up to Him.

OF CONFERENCES AND KINGS

"The time has come," the Walrus said,
"To talk of many things:
Of shoes—and ships—and sealing-wax—
Of cabbages—and kings—
And why the sea is boiling hot—
And whether pigs have wings."

Lewis Carroll

A well-known interrogation technique involves giving a suspect a friendly drink of water or coffee. As the questioning goes on, the interrogator shares even more water or coffee. Friendly, you know, since this will take a while. Only... the suspect is never given the chance to go to the bathroom.

Have you ever tried to think, to be creative, with a bladder so full you think you've developed six-pack abs?

I'm convinced this is why Robin, conference director and a fabulous writer of suspense novels, plops huge vessels of water near the interrog—um—*appointment* rooms at the American Christian Fiction Writers conference.

"Yes, YES, I'll take a look at your manuscript. Here's my card. Now get out of the way. The bathroom is all the way on the other side of the hotel..."

Well, maybe not.

Several years ago, around 2008, if memory serves, I stopped by my mother's home on the way back from the annual gathering of the ACFW. When my mother asked me what I did at the conference, I responded, "I talked. And I listened. Then I talked some more. About many things."

Of shoes—and ships—and sealing-wax...

On Friday, I spent most of the day with agents and friends. Often, these are one and the same. I've been doing this for a long time, past the time when colleagues become close friends. We talked trends and clients and publisher needs. Is my publisher still interested in Amish? (Not for a year or so.) Will Amish still lead the industry? (Maybe, but it's evolving and developing cross-genre interests—this was 2008.) What about speculative? (Still looking for a really good one.) Women's fiction...and so on.

Everyone seemed to be aware of two things: The industry is *always* in an evolving state, but people are less panicky about it. Publishers are adjusting and finding new ways to deal with the changes, although sometimes those changes take a while to implement.

And why the sea is boiling hot...

The big question (as it always has been) is about discoverability—getting books to readers. As with everything else, this is constantly evolving and is becoming more genre specific. No concrete method exists...but there has *never* been a concrete method

of reaching readers, despite the moaning for the "good ol' days" of publisher advertising and bookstore presence.

Books on *Oprah*, or *The Late Show*, or *Good Morning, America* don't always leap into readers' hands, despite that exposure. The same with major book clubs. Sometimes being a book club pick means instant fame. More often...not. Endorsements from best-selling authors don't always work either. Good reviews of a new Robert Galbraith suspense book didn't equate sales until the author turned out to be J. K. Rowling in disguise.

But lest you think that's a new phenomenon, remember that a certain suspense book sold less than 4,000 copies until Ronald Reagan praised Tom Clancy for the details in *The Hunt for Red October*. Likewise, Ian Fleming's little spy series only sold moderately well until the author met with President Kennedy.

Unfortunately, most of us don't have presidents at hand to promote our books.

So...trends and needs and numbers...all floating in my head when I spent two days taking appointments. I talked to more than sixty authors in scheduled appointments and impromptu meetings at meals, in hallways...and, yes, in the elevator. Of those, I asked to see about forty manuscripts once they're finished. I expect to receive about ten. Maybe. Receipt of 25 percent of requests is actually a bit high for conference requests.

The themes for the books ranged from suspense and politics to contemporary and historical romance. I had questions for most of the authors, and I found most of the premises intriguing. In the end, some will fit and be well written enough for me to buy. Most won't.

What I hope is that no matter what comes in life or from publishers, these folks will persevere and keep writing. *And* keep attending conferences. *This* book may not be the one that gets picked up by a president, but you never know what God has planned for the next one—or your life.

You see, a few years ago, I stalked an editor at a conference. She finally agreed to look at my resume and gave me a chance to line edit for her company, then write back cover copy. It meant my toe in the door. When I was ready, their team knew me when I submitted a book proposal. And they bought it. The result was my first book with Love Inspired Suspense, *A Murder Among Friends*, which is still selling in e-book format. Six books later, *Memory of Murder* received the most reviews of any of my LIS books, and I hope I can continue to write for them.

But it also directly led to me being considered for the job of fiction editor for Abingdon Press. My dream job. Which I finally landed at the age of fifty-three.

So never give up. Because you have no idea if one day God will allow porcine liftoff.

And whether pigs have wings.

Reflections on Being a Princess, or How Writing Conferences Look Like Cinderella's Kingdom

People say, "What advice do you have for people who want to be writers?" I say, they don't really need advice, they know they want to be writers, and they're gonna do it. Those people who know that they really want to do this and are cut out for it, they know it.

R. L. Stine, *Writer's Digest*

When I was a kid, that blonde girl in the long, blue dress seemed to be everywhere.

Cinderella. That irrepressibly optimistic teenager covered movie posters, lunchboxes, toys. I even received a Cinderella watch as a present, complete with the ceramic doll that sat on my dresser, well out of bumping range. (I was and am a klutz.)

Well, OK, not so successfully out of bumping range (yes…klutz). Chasing imaginary horses around my room one rainy afternoon led me to collide with the dresser. Cindy bounced off her perch, skidded across the Pledge-polished wood, and landed on the floor with an unfortunate snap. Thereafter, she spent life with a yellowish glue line around her middle, a symbol of my mother's "if it breaks, fix it!" attitude.

We didn't throw much away in those days. We weren't hoarders; my mother always kept a spotless, uncluttered house. We just weren't a family who bought much, and when we did buy something, it had to last. We made do. So broken dolls were fixed, and a cast-off telephone cable reel took up residence in our backyard to stand in for horses, airplanes, forts, and any number of World War II front lines. (Yes, I had a big brother.)

So I didn't fuss too much about a broken ceramic doll. Of course, I never was too attached to Cindy to start with. I didn't "get" Cinderella. The prince was cute and that party looked like fun, but her ordinary life reminded me a little too much of our everyday chores for me to be truly distraught for her. Plus, she had birds and soft, furry things to play with.

Like I did. Cats and dogs, and for a while a robin that got tangled in a cat's cradle of string my brother had left in the backyard. I was definitely more prone to reenact the adventures of Robin Kane and her palomino or Nancy Drew and her friend George than I was to play with dolls. Oh, and Amelia Earhart. Loved the strength of these women—the adventures!—and not many of them had a prince tagging along to get in the way.

Nope, if I wanted to be a princess, it wouldn't involve parties and elegant dresses. It would involve adventures. And most of all, it would involve *books*!

As an adult, this would translate into writers conferences, where I would be treated like a princess. Yeah. Six days as a princess. My kind of princess.

Start with a fairy tale setting, such as northern California. Well more than a century old, the Mount Hermon Conference Center is nestled in the California mountains. Rustic-looking cabins, inns, meeting halls, chapels, and auditoriums dot odd-sized open spaces between the towering redwoods. The sidewalks and trails undulate with the rise and fall of steep hillsides. Arching bridges, flowering cherry trees and aza-lea and camellia bushes, and meandering streams lined with ferns and emerald vines add to the storylike atmosphere. The air is cool and moist, and moss grows on stones embedded into walkways decades ago.

Throw into this setting 250 or so people who love books. **Love** them. Want to talk about them: about reading them, learning from them, writing them, publishing them. All types, all genres of books. These are my people, my tribe.

I felt very much like a princess must feel. People wanted to ask me questions and often complimented me. I love teaching, and my classes were packed. I only hope the conferees enjoyed the classes as much as I did and gleaned something from my ram-blings. I was served fabulous food that I didn't have to cook (or clean up after). I sat at the feet of (OK, no—across the table from)

those who know a lot more than I do and absorbed their knowledge like a starving bird.

I learned as much as I taught, getting a chance to swap stories and information with agents, editors, and publishers. I participated in worship with one of the best-singing congregations I've heard in a long time. People loved on me and on each other. I felt pampered and praised.

I could get used to that.

So, you might ask, other than the setting, what makes Mount Hermon different from other conferences I've attended?

To be honest? Not much. The conference is longer, but like at other great conferences, it's crammed with professional-level courses geared toward taking writers of all levels and pushing them toward publication. Twice I heard the conference described as "a graduate-level crash course in publishing," which could apply to most of these intense gatherings of writers. After all, almost all writers conferences are engineered to teach, encourage, and uplift writers. Even experienced writers learn from each other, and the mentoring that goes on in the small, impromptu groups can change careers, if not lives. There are dozens of excellent conferences each year, probably one near you. So if you are serious about your words, I highly recommend that you "Get thee to a writers conference!"

When I wrote this, I was 38,000 feet over New Mexico, about 1,100 miles from home (according to the pilot). It was 9:30 p.m., and the only light I could see was the one on the wingtip. I had passed "tired" about 3 p.m. two days earlier. "Wired and brain-fried" arrived early that morning. And (yet another indication that I'm not really cut out to be a princess) I've been horribly homesick

this trip, an unusual occurrence for this adventure-prone lover of books and travel.

But underneath the exhaustion and the home-longing is that I want to get back to my friends and my work. My work as an editor and a writer. Playing princess is fun and inspiring, but I am—like Cinderella before the fairy tale—a servant at heart. My work is a gift from God, and I love being His servant. Time to turn that "crash course" into "His course."

It's a familiar feeling to anyone who's attended a great writer's conference.

WHAT THEY SAW

More than any other factor, it is the people we have to deal with that determine the quality of our work lives.

David H. Master, *True Professionalism*

Conference pitches are always a time of nerves and questioning. It's unknown territory for most people, as they have no idea how the agents and editors will respond to their ideas and hopes.

I was at the Blue Ridge Mountains Christian Writers Conference in 2016, this time as a mentor. I talked to a lot of shaky young writers, just to give them advice on what steps to take next. During one of my last appointments, a young woman sat down, her face clouded in puzzlement. She introduced herself and said, "Can I talk to you about something?"

"Sure. What's up?"

Her hands were shaking as she took out her one-sheets and handed me a business card. She pitched two ideas in just under three minutes. I looked at her and said, "These sound marvelous. So what do you want from me?"

She looked over her shoulder, then leaned in to explain. She'd pitched to sixteen editors and agents, and every single one of them had asked for a full manuscript. She thought that was odd—everyone had warned her it would be tough in this market. So she had two main questions. Was it strange to get so many requests? And with that many, who should she start with?

"This is a good problem to have," I said. "But, first, let me explain what people are seeing when you sit in front of them."

- **She had a polished and professional appearance.** This is more important than some people would like to admit. While writers don't have to be pretty or handsome, they do need to be clean and neatly dressed in appropriate attire.

- **She had her materials ready and well prepared.** She handed me her business card, and her one-sheets were well designed and communicated her message clearly. Her bio pinpointed her platform, background in her field, and past experiences as a speaker.

- **Her ideas were unique and well presented.** She had a passion, a strong enthusiasm for her works, and sold them with joy. And she *knew* her ideas were unique because...

- **She knew her market, and included in her presentation ideas for reaching them.** She didn't ramble or present a broad audience. She knew exactly who she wanted to reach with her books.

- **She had more than one idea to present.** While agents and editors obviously are in the market to buy one project, they also keep an eye out for authors who are interested in

building a career. Their best efforts go into an author who wants to do this as a profession.

- **She asked questions beyond "Do you want my book?"** She wanted to know what other types of clients the agents had, and she'd researched the editors to know what they buy.

As I rattled off the litany of reasons she'd make a good client for an agent or author for an editor, her eyes widened. She had no idea that she was hitting all the sweet spots. **She was simply trying to be as professional and as prepared as possible.** She succeeded—and the agents and editors spotted it right away.

I spread her one-sheets in front of me, and made suggestions on which agents or editors might be a good fit for her. I also suggested that she find a couple of authors who worked with them and have a chat. Every agent and editor is different, and making a good personality and career-focus match is vital for long-term success.

Pitches are stressful, but being prepared can alleviate some nerves. Presenting a professional appearance takes little time and can have encouraging results. It costs nothing to bathe and put on clean clothes. Comb your hair. Read over your pitches until you can deliver them with enthusiasm and few stutters. Be on time for your appointment, and leave when your time is up.

We may hear this over and over, but you might be surprised to know how few people come to the table ready to present. The ones who do prepare stand out. And that's what made this young author shine for a roomful of agents and editors.

AFTER THE FIRE HOSE

It gets harder to write novels, not easier.

Jonathan Franzen

I t's been compared to drinking from a fire hose. It's been called "graduate school in a week." It's intense, in-depth, and incomparable. It's also a remarkable amount of fun.

It's a writers conference. Whether in one day or a week, a great conference can change your life and your career. You will leave enthused, engaged, and encouraged. Of course, if you've been there, you already know this. If you haven't been, think seriously how important a conference can be to your writing, your personal network, and your future.

But how do you deal with the fire hose, the aftermath of "graduate school in a week"? After the euphoria of engaging with your own people—writers—what happens when you get home?

Well, what happens first tends to be a feeling of overwhelmed exhaustion. The blues. A fog. A slump. A miasma, if you're feeling word nerdy. *Lost.*

All of these words have been used by writers to describe the days following a writers conference. Oh, at first, there's pure exhilaration, an energy burst that comes from the days of brainstorming, classes that spark the imagination, sudden friendships formed from faith and familiarity. The rush home, the joy of trying to explain all that's happened. Ideas blossom, begging to get written.

Then...finally...sleep.

But the enthusiasm is bordered by a stunned emotional exhaustion. Even after your body has rested, your mind and heart may feel overpowered and confused by the amount of information you received and the gang of friends you made. They all weigh heavily as you want to write and put everything in action.

If you can only decide where and how to start. Yet before any of the ideas from the conference can be implemented, the daily routine returns. Work, house, family crowd in, glad to have you back. By the way, do you remember that we need to go...do you remember where this is...we need to.... Demands that are real and necessary swoop back over you, and the elation of the conference fades. You begin to think you'll never be able to implement all you've learned.

But you will.

Because you have a call on your life like no other.

In many ways, a writers conference is a fantasy world, and when real life sets in again, the blues from leaving that fantasy world behind can be exacerbated. In addition to the post-conference slump, you can started to believe that all the dreams borne from that time will never see fruition. But they will, because your call to write won't be ignored. So after the elation—and the slump—it's

time to settle back in and call on the discipline that'll make it happen.

Discipline. How we writers sometimes hate that word. It smacks of work. But writing *is* work. Hard work.

There's a strange notion that floats around that writing is easy. You have an idea; write it down. Simple. And that part is.

But being an author is much more than writing down ideas. It's about *communicating* those ideas to a wide readership; conforming work to standards most readers use and publishers require. It's about knowing the psychology of the human mind and how we perceive stories. It's about adapting and using the best vocabulary for that audience. It's about understanding story structure, character development, plot devices, and methods of building suspense. It's about writing, editing, rewriting, and smoothing every passage until it shines. And it's also about knowing when to let go and sending your creation out into the world...for judgment.

Hard work. Something else to get the blues about.

Here are a few tips on processing the aftermath, fighting all the blues of transition, and getting back on track. They may, in fact, help you plan for the *next* conference. Because once you have a great conference experience, you'll want another. I won't say they're addicting, but....

- **Take a breath and get some more sleep.** Seriously. I know you'll want to dive into productivity, but give yourself a break. What you're going through is natural. Don't fight it. Get some rest and hug your loved ones. Rest a few more days. Plan before you ever go to the conference to do so,

and let your family and friends know you're going to need some time to sort everything out. This will also help when the everyday routine begins to crash back in on you.

- **Pray.** Open a conversation and seek His guidance on your writing and the direction He wants you to take. It'll be way too easy to want to *do it all right now!* Don't. Listen first.

- **Stew on what you've learned.** Review your notes; listen to the recordings, if available. *Do not* try to recapture the elation. Let that go. But this review can remind you of the good and valuable things you learned. Let them ferment and become part of your writing mindset. This will also give you time to readjust to the daily demands. Don't *force* yourself to start implementing things.

- **Make a list of short-term and long-term goals.** *Short-term goals* (to be completed in the next month or so) may involve things like sending thank you notes to editors and agents who asked for more information—or just for taking the time to list what was most valuable to you about the conference. Making social media connections. Updating those pages to be more professional. Reviewing your website. *Long-term goals* will include items like new dates for completing a book or a series of articles. Setting the number of submissions you want to make next month and developing a plan to do so. Oh...and actually submitting that manuscript the agent asked for.

- **Start (or expand) an "idea bucket."** Whether you use a device or paper to capture ideas, start a new file of bits and bytes, fleeting ideas that hit you in the middle of traffic, or the shower, or in church when the sermon sparks something to remember (not that we ever let our minds wander

in church...). One of the biggest lies writers tell themselves is "Oh, I'll remember that."

- **Slowly reestablish your writing routine.** Like the rest of your activities, a writers conference has disrupted your world. Settle back in. Write some test pieces. If you're in the middle of a work-in-progress, read it again from the beginning with your new information in mind.

- **Implement new information while editing.** *But* don't think you suddenly have to change the way you write. You don't. Much of what you learned is best implemented when you *edit*. Trying to change the way you get a story down on paper can often derail your process. The more you *edit* with the new information, the more it will become ingrained in your head. Little by little, you'll discover that you write with it...but don't push it. Becoming a better writer is a process in itself. Don't try to dictate it. Let it grow naturally from the way you absorb and implement new information.

- **Network.** There's nothing like the support and comfort of other writers to build you up. If one of your goals involves connecting with a writing group, look into the ones already available (like WordWeavers) or consider starting your own. Check out the frequent tips about increasing your social media presence. Engage!

How do you drink from a firehose? With careful planning. One sip at a time.

Most of all, trust yourself and your gift. And God. He gave it to you. He'll lead you through it.

It's Just Ol'
What's-Her-Name

O day of days when we can read!
The reader and the book,
either without the other is naught.

Ralph Waldo Emerson

I used to keep a wig in my office. No, not for bad hair days. "She" was on a stand, and sticky notes cluttered the base of it, documenting her age, profession, income, background, church activity, family, and buying habits. Her name was Nancy.

She was my audience.

Back then, I was acquiring and editing non-dated curriculum: DVDs and study guides. And while the details have changed somewhat, I still keep Nancy in mind as I acquire and write fiction.

How do we determine who Nancy truly is? This information has many sources. Publishers get some advice from a company that studies the market constantly through publisher and consumer

surveys. We also watch social media, follow readers groups, talk to authors about what they're hearing at signings, book clubs, and in social media groups. We do focus groups and title testing, and we track the responses. This is the essence of the business end of what we do. I look for the best books I can find, but in addition to the quality of the work, I have to ask myself: "Can I reach Nancy or her friends with it? How would I do that with *this* book?"

So when the information, including thousands of survey responses, is broken down, who is Nancy? Who buys Christian fiction?

The majority:

- Are women (thus she's Nancy, not Norman)
- Have a household income of less than $50,000 per year (keep this figure in mind)
- Are 45 years old or older
- Are active (church every week plus involvement) or professing (church occasionally) Christians
- Spend only 3 percent or so of their book-buying money for Christian fiction

And the number-one way they *discover* new books and spend that limited amount of money is through the recommendation of a friend. **Word of mouth.** Readers beget readers. They still enjoy bookstores, but online presence (through author's website, blogs, or retailer promotions) is the also a major area of visibility. And primary reason for *buying* (which is different from how they discover a book) is author recognition. The second is interest in a series or genre.

So what do writers do with this information? Well, there's good news and bad news here. But the best thing a writer can do is to be prepared and have realistic expectations about working in this field.

The Takeaways

- Reaching the reader is *key*. Spend time with other writers and craft blogs to learn, but abandon the idea that networking with other writers is going to generate sales. Not unless that networking is putting you in touch with other writers' *readers*.

- Brick-and-mortar stores are not dead; they're just not dominant anymore. That's why so many are closing. But a lot of print books are still being bought through stores. Folks still love putting their hands on the product before they buy. Will that change? Probably. But for now, developing and maintaining a relationship with a store remains a good idea.

- This demographic—Nancy—will continue to drive acquisitions and buy-ins—what editors purchase and what retail buyers add to their inventory. If you're already writing for Nancy, your promotional paths are a bit more established, but your competition is stiffer. More authors in Christian publishing write for her than don't.

- If you are *not* writing for Nancy, your publishing options are more limited, but the field is more open, especially as more and more readers embrace the growth in review sites and other online marketing avenues. You need to look closely at your readers, who they are, and find ways

to reach them. Nancy may be the majority of the audience, but she's not the *only* audience. Be open to new promotional ideas, like launch teams.

- Ebooks seem to be leveling out at about 20–25 percent of the market as of 2020. This was expected. There will be exceptions, and that number will fluctuate. But no one sees ebooks becoming dominant anytime soon. One reason for this is that people still use readers primarily for their convenience: on the train, traveling, coffee shops, etc. For pure leisure reading at home, they're still turning to print.

Everything I've heard in the past few years is grounded in optimism, even as the marketplace continues to shift and flow. While we are still undergoing a sea change in the industry and the learning curve continues, the waters are smoother and more familiar, even as new territories await. It's up to you to explore the old as well as the new.

REVIEWING REVIEWS

How a human being could have attempted such a book as the present without committing suicide before he had finished a dozen chapters, is a mystery. It is a compound of vulgar depravity and unnatural horrors.

Review of *Wuthering Heights*, 1848

They are the psyche killers of every author. They will break your heart and make you cry. They will make you want to quit writing and move to Siberia. They will make you doubt the gift you know, without a doubt, is from God.

Negative reviews. The reviews that cut to the quick; the ones that declare you to be a horrible writer. The ones that proclaim your best-wrought prose to be a shameful failure of the most mortifying kind.

When one pops up in front of your face, your chest and stomach tighten until you can't breathe. You immediately have a flash of anger and a driving desire to fight back, to post a response, to tell all your friends to pile on this reviewer with both feet. Whether

it's on a blog, a retail site, or in a magazine, the natural human response would be to defend your art, your craft...your gift.

This would be a mistake. Just stop and take five or six deep breaths. Or seventy-times-seven.

DON'T DO THIS

- *Do NOT respond,* even if the review is wrong about something in the book. Horror stories abound about authors who engage critics over a single review, often making the *authors* look petty, foolish, and immature as people as well as writers. That kind of battle can not only lose readers but future editors as well.

- *Don't email your editor or publicist about it.* They probably already know about it, and while they'll sympathize (it reflects on them as well), they can't do anything about it.

DO THIS INSTEAD

- *Remember: While everyone has an opinion, they aren't all relevant.* Your book was written with a specific audience in mind (remember Nancy?), and people have a lot of differing tastes. I'm currently reading a book, for instance, by a best-selling romance author. *Mega*-selling author. A "starred review" in a major magazine, and 4.5 stars from another. And already I've rolled my eyes so much the over-the-top prose, clichéd characters, and vintage plot that I have a headache. Some of the Amazon reviews have called the book "tedious," "boring," and "overwhelming." My guess is the author is ignoring them all the way to the bank.

Just because a reader doesn't enjoy your book does not mean the book is badly written. I am not, obviously, the audience for the book I was reading, even though I read romantic suspense. But a review that doesn't offer much other than "this is a horrible book" offers up an unsupported opinion that's of value to neither the author nor other readers.

- *The criticism could, in fact, be enticing to some readers.* If the critic hits the book because it's "too Christian," they've noticed something most of your intended readers will embrace. A romance criticized for being "too sentimental" or "fluffy," may be just what a potential reader may be looking for in a novel. Some critics try to lend weight to their opinions by insulting any reader who likes the book: "Anyone who likes this book is an idiot." But readers will form their own opinion. The influence of a review only goes so far.

- *Review the review—and learn from it.* Negative reviews that are well written, however, could offer up criticism that could help your writing improve. A review that complains about character development may also include hints about where that went wrong. In one of my earlier books, I received a review that criticized the heroine's behavior in a critical scene. After the sting wore off, I realized that the reviewer had not understood my heroine because I hadn't done my job building her life and backstory. It was a mistake I've tried to avoid ever since.

- *Focus on the positives about the book and the review process.* Few books receive universally negative reviews, and even negative reviews often include positive points. Although

it *is* "easier to believe the bad stuff," recognize that the positive remarks about your book underline that you do have a gift and that you are using it well. Keep a running list of positive words about your book. They make a great reminder the next time you write yourself into a corner.

- **You are not alone.** The greatest authors in the world receive negative reviews. Like rejections, every writer receives them sooner or later. They are part of the business you've chosen to join. No job in the world is all sunshine and roses, and if you do it long enough and you publish enough, the negative thorns will occasionally pop up. Learn what you can from them, and then, in Elsa's words: "Let It Go."

I often want to criticize Jane Austen, but her books madden me so that I can't conceal my frenzy from the reader; and therefore I have to stop every time I begin. Every time I read Pride and Prejudice *I want to dig her up and beat her over the skull with her own shin-bone!*

Mark Twain

WHAT TO DO WHEN YOU WIN A MAJOR AWARD—AND WHEN YOU DON'T

My mother used to tell me man gives the award; God gives the reward.

Denzel Washington

The year 2015 was a banner one for Abingdon Press when it comes to winning awards. Among others, their books received the following:

- One Christy: Ace Collins, *The Color of Justice*
- Seven Christian Retailing Best Awards, one for fiction: Cynthia Ruchti, *All My Belongings*
- Four IndieFab awards from ForeWord magazine, three for fiction: Deb Raney, *Home to Chicory Lane*; Sharyn McCrumb, *Nora Bonesteel's Christmas Past*; and Cynthia Ruchti, *All My Belongings*

- Three AWSA awards: for Deb, Cynthia, and Eva Marie Everson's *The Road to Testament*
- The Gayle Wilson Award for Excellence for Deb
- ACFW Carol nominations for Lisa Carter and Jennifer Allee...and for me, as Editor of the Year

Yet, in a year for which these were praised, Abingdon's fiction program published thirty-two books. What about all those other titles? Weren't they as good? Weren't they worthy of acclaim?

Of course, they were. Many more books deserve awards than get them. That's just a fact of life. So how does an author make the most of winning? And what do you do if you were nominated but lost? Or not even recognized at all?

Obviously, there are marketing angles you can pursue if you win... working with your publisher on a press release, adding notices to your website and social media pages. If you have a relationship with a local bookstore, let the manager know you've picked up an award.

But the best advice I can give to winners is to be gracious. Don't overdo the humility (that's a little grating), but give simple and honest thanks and appreciation to those who congratulate you. You worked hard to get there...don't pass it off as though this isn't an important part of your journey. It is, and there's no reason you shouldn't acknowledge it.

Don't dwell on it, however. You've won. Excellent. Celebrate! Then move on to your next project. You still have work to do!

And if you were nominated but didn't win...also make use of this recognition. Believe me, no one sees you as a "loser." Instead, you

wrote a fabulous book that caught readers' attention with the quality of the story and the craft. The same with the books that received second or third place. Embrace the acclaim, spread it around a little, then move on.

But what if you didn't even get a blink from an award committee? Again, be gracious. Send kind congratulations, and celebrate with your fellow authors. These are your friends. They deserve your support and happiness for them. After all...as Jesse Owens once said, "Awards become corroded, friends gather no dust."

Remember: awards lift *all* of us up in a way, reminding readers that we're still here and still writing. And readers *will* watch to see how you react to your peers' success. They care.

And don't despair or fall into the trap of thinking you're not good enough. Ace Collins has written more than sixty books... this was his first *nomination* for a Christy, as well as his first win. Deb Raney has written more than thirty books. If Ace or Deb had been discouraged by not winning awards, where would they be now? And I've been editing for almost forty years—and I didn't win that award in 2015. But I'm still editing great books.

The bottom line is that, as nice as they are, **awards do not tell you who you are**. Or who you aren't. That message only comes from one Source...and it's not an awards committee.

STILL JUST ONE EDITOR'S OPINION

Write. Remember, people may keep you (or me) from being a published author, but no one can stop you from being a writer. All you have to do is write.

Katherine Neville

So I was talking to a friend today, and she asked a half dozen questions about this book. "Well, did you talk about?..." "So did you mention?..."

My answers to her questions were all the same: "No." Because this is not, and I never intended it to be, an exhaustive look at writing and editing. I have a bookshelf overflowing with books on the craft of writing, and they only scratch the surface. A brief search online would review a hundred more—some excellent, some not worth the cash.

This book was intended as personal reflections on the industry after traveling through it for the past forty years. While everyone's experience with writing and publishing differs, I hope that

I've offered some advice and direction, and I hope some guidance and encouragement for whatever you're dealing with on your own writing journey.

But I'm still just one opinion among hundreds. And the publishing industry changes daily. Self-publishing is a mixed bag, as far as success rates go, but more authors are finding it suits them and their work. Today's trends are tomorrow's nostalgia. And that goes for anything I've said in the book.

The bottom line goes back to some of the best advice I ever received, and it's absolutely timeless, unfazed by trends and market changes.

In late 1970s, I got the opportunity to ride from Murfreesboro, Tennessee, to the Nashville airport with Harlan Ellison. I was a nervous fangirl. Despite his reputation, he was gracious as I tried not to gush over him. I mentioned I had a "friend" who wanted to write like him. He smiled gently as he responded, and I knew he'd heard that a million times before.

"No. Tell your 'friend' that she doesn't need to write like me. She has her own voice and her own stories to tell. She needs to find that voice and tell those stories. And never give up. If she's a real writer, and even those stories wind up in a drawer, she will never give up. A writer has to write."

Obviously, I don't write like Harlan Ellison, and my career trajectory is about as far from his as I could possibly get. But I never forgot his words. Or his grace with a novice.

So, if you're a writer, go write. And never give up.

ACKNOWLEDGMENTS

I definitely did not arrive at this place alone.

From Bonnie S. Calhoun, who encouraged me to write a monthly column the very first time, to Edie Melson, who encouraged me to continue to do so for the Blue Ridge Mountains Christian Writers Conference, to Eva Marie Everson, who considers me "the source" for all things grammar, my network of encouragers is treasured and immense. They are writing sisters who've walked difficult journeys of their own, emerging with success due to hard work and dependence on God's guidance.

Thanks also go to Kristen Stieffel and Reagan Jackson, who completed masterful edits on this, and my entire ISM team: John, Bradley, Reagan, Tina, Meredith, Randy, and Marty. They ground me and keep me moving forward.

The ivory tower with a writer scribbling away all alone is a myth. For which I'm eternally grateful.

References and Resources

The number of resources for writers is extensive. Obviously, I've not read them all—most I have no acquaintance with at all. Ask writers about their favorite resources, and you'll get a different list for each one. The ones here are those I have used and trust. They are meant to be a starting point and not an all-inclusive list.

That said, the first one on the list (*CMOS 17*) is an essential text for everyone who wants to pursue writing as more than an occasional hobby. You can also subscribe to it online, which means it's searchable. Well worth the price for either the subscription or print.

Also, Writer's Digest Books published a series called Write Great Fiction. I've listed a couple of the titles below, but the entire series is well done and provides an excellent basis for a craft library.

Books

The Chicago Manual of Style, 17th edition. Chicago: University of Chicago Press, 2017.

Bell, James Scott. *The Art of War for Writers.* Cincinnati: Writer's Digest Books, 2009.

Brown, Renni, and Dave King. *Self-Editing for Fiction Writers.* New York: William Morrow Paperbacks, 2004.

Card, Orson Scott. *Characters & Viewpoint.* Elements of Fiction Writing series. Cincinnati: Writer's Digest Books, 1988.

Collins, Brandilyn. *Getting Into Character: Seven Secrets A Novelist Can Learn From Actors, 2nd edition.* Coeur d'Alene, ID: Challow Press, 2015.

Friedman, Jane. *The Business of Being a Writer.* Chicago: University of Chicago Press, 2018.

Jordan, Robert. *The Christian Writer's Manual of Style, 4th edition.* Grand Rapids: Zondervan, 2016.

Ingermanson, Randall. *How to Write a Novel Using the Snowflake Method.* Ingermanson Communications, 2014.

James, Steven. *Story Trumps Structure: How to Write Unforgettable Fiction by Breaking the Rules.* Cincinnati: Writer's Digest Books, 2014.

James, Steven. *Troubleshooting Your Novel: Essential Techniques for Identifying and Solving Manuscript Problems.* Cincinnati: Writer's Digest Books, 2016.

King, Stephen. *On Writing: A Memoir of the Craft.* New York: Pocket Books, 2000.

Rozelle, Ron. *Description & Setting.* Write Great Fiction series. Cincinnati: Writer's Digest Books, 2005.

Blogs

Again, writing blogs abound. I suggest doing a search and try out a few, especially those geared toward your genre or interest.

If you self-publish, blogs that advise and guide can be helpful, but networking with other writers might be more beneficial. As always, read several posts, see if they are a fit for what you do. These are a few that I've found useful. They were all accessed on January 14, 2020, but with the internet, sites come and go.

Between the Lines/Books & Such Literary Agency
https://www.booksandsuch.com/blog/

Nathan Bransford
https://blog.nathanbransford.com/

Jane Friedman
https://www.janefriedman.com/blog/

The Kill Zone
https://killzoneblog.com/

Jerry Jenkins
https://jerryjenkins.com/blog/

The Passive Voice
https://www.thepassivevoice.com/

Seekerville
https://seekerville.blogspot.com/

Steve Laube Agency Blog
https://stevelaube.com/blog/

The Write Conversation/Edie Melson
https://thewriteconversation.blogspot.com/

The Writing Life/Terry Whalin
http://terrywhalin.blogspot.com/

ABOUT THE AUTHOR

The author of eleven books, Ramona Richards has worked on staff or as a freelancer for more than a dozen publishers and has edited more than 500 publications. She's stated that she'll edit anything as long as it's not illegal, and over her career has advised and worked with authors of novels, trade nonfiction on a variety of topics, magazine articles, sales training videos, websites, blogs, cookbooks, biographies, memoirs, Bibles and Bible studies, CD-ROMs, screenplays, and air conditioning repair manuals. She is now associate publisher at Iron Stream Media, the parent company of New Hope Publishers and LPC Books.

In 2019, Ramona received the Joann Sloan National Award for the Encouragement of Writing, a mentoring, editing, and coaching award presented by Vision Press at the Southern Christian Writers Conference. She is also a frequent speaker at writer's conferences around the country, and the Advanced Writers and Speakers Association nominated her for Best Editor of the Year in 2008 and the Best Fiction Editor of the Year in 2013.

A member of American Christian Fiction Writers and the Advanced Writers and Speakers Association, Ramona lives in Moody, Alabama, but can be found online at these locations:

LinkedIn: ramonarichards
Facebook: ramona.richards
Twitter: @RamonaRichards
Instagram: @ramonapoperichards

**If you enjoyed this book, will you consider sharing
the message with others?**

Let us know your thoughts at info@newhopepublishers.com. You
can also let the author know by visiting or sharing a photo of the
cover on our social media pages or leaving a review at a retailer's
site. All of it helps us get the message out!

Twitter.com/NewHopeBooks
Facebook.com/NewHopePublishers
Instagram.com/NewHopePublishers

New Hope® Publishers, Ascender Books, Iron Stream Books,
and New Hope Kidz are imprints of Iron Stream Media,
which derives its name from Proverbs 27:17,

"As iron sharpens iron, so one person sharpens another."

This sharpening describes the process of discipleship, one to
another. With this in mind, Iron Stream Media provides a variety
of solutions for churches, ministry leaders, and nonprofits ranging
from in-depth Bible study curriculum and Christian book
publishing to custom publishing and consultative services.
Through the popular Life Bible Study and Student Life Bible Study
brands, ISM provides web-based full-year and short-term Bible
study teaching plans as well as printed devotionals, Bibles, and
discipleship curriculum.

For more information on ISM and New Hope Publishers,
please visit
IronStreamMedia.com
NewHopePublishers.com

The **essential go-to tool** for aspiring and experienced writers and editors.

Available from ShopLPC.com and your favorite book retailers

Editing Secrets of Best-Selling Authors is an excellent resource, especially for aspiring authors hoping to turn professional.

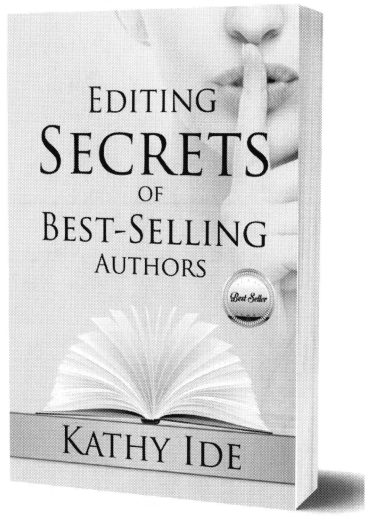

Available from ShopLPC.com and your favorite book retailers

TRACKING
CHANGES